Ready For Anything

Designing Resilience for a Transforming World

Anthony Hodgson

International Futures Forum

Published by:
Triarchy Press
Station Offices
Axminster
Devon. EX13 5PF
United Kingdom

+44 (0)1297 631456
info@triarchypress.com
www.triarchypress.com

© International Futures Forum, 2011

The right of Anthony Hodgson to be identified as the author of this book has been asserted by him in accordance with the Copyright, Designs and Patents Act, 1988.

A catalogue record for this book is available from the British Library.

ISBN:978-1-908009-46-3

International Futures Forum

The Boathouse
Silversands
Hawkcraig Road
Aberdour
Fife KY3 0TZ
Scotland
Tel +44 (0)1383 861300
www.internationalfuturesforum.com

Man is a prisoner of his own way of thinking
and of his own stereotypes of himself.
His machine for thinking
the brain
has been programmed to deal with a vanished world.
This old world was characterized by the need
to manage things –
stone, wood, iron.
The new world is characterized by the need
to manage
complexity.
Complexity is the very stuff of today's world.

Stafford Beer, *Platform for Change*

... all those who have the spark of the explorer, the
discoverer, the risk-taker – the learner. For those who
go through the swamp or up the mountain because they
are made that way. These are the people we shall have to
count on to face the appalling issues described here, to set
the goals and try to reach them, and to learn from their
failures and successes and go on trying and learning.

Alexander King and Bertrand Schneider,
The First Global Revolution

Contents

Preface

Books about the state of the world and its future are now commonplace. As the skies turn dark, and one inconvenient truth piles on top of another, most such books are stories of impending doom and collapse – wake-up calls for a threatened planet. Others are more positive, challenging the pessimism of the doom-mongers and promising a rich human future – always with the caveat that we must first *summon the collective wisdom necessary to change course.*

This book falls into neither category. It pulls no punches about the state of our global predicament – which is indeed serious and threatening. Tony Hodgson remarks that we have coped so far with occasional devastating interruptions to business as usual, early warnings. But this is a world in which we are forever on the brink of 'synchronous failure' – where one thing triggers another and amplifies a third – that will eventually lead to a crisis beyond our capacity to contain or to recover.

Rather than deliver another blueprint for what we *must do* in these circumstances and how urgently we *must do it* in order to fend off disaster and save civilisation, Hodgson's offer in this book is both more modest and more profound.

Our much missed friend and IFF[1] colleague the late Max Boisot used to suggest that the wisdom of an action is proportionate to the depth and breadth of context that informs it. If the challenge is to manage the implications of 7 billion people living together on a single planet, therefore, the context we need to take into account ideally needs to span the globe. That, almost by definition, is impossible – but Hodgson argues we can do a whole lot better than the reductionist, rationalist, silo-bunkered mental models we rely on at the moment.

The World System Model provides a deceptively simple way to frame our decisions in the context of everything that is going on in the world. On one level it acts as a scanning framework – for significant global trends, promising innovations, potential disruptions. The comprehensive nature of the model makes even this basic function valuable, going as it does far beyond the usual 'STEEP' framework (society, technology, economy, environment, politics). It broadens the context for our decision-making, eliminates blind spots, highlights connections. And because it is based on the fundamentals of a viable socio-ecological system it is valid at all levels - from globe to village, nation to family.

But its real value lies at a deeper level. For it also encourages in us new capacities to make sense of what would otherwise be overwhelming, confusing, contradictory data about the state of the world today and tomorrow. Hodgson describes the World System Model as 'a cognitive gymnasium', 'a mandala', as the basis for a role-playing 'World Game' and – in its playground version – '21st century hopscotch'. We may not be able to analyse our way through the mass of data about the world, but the Model at least gives us a way to engage with it. And through that engagement we overcome our fear of the complexity – 'it's all too much for me' – and start revelling in its potential. It is this quality that makes the Model so effective as 'a platform for deeply informed, pragmatic world visioning'.

Hodgson shows how the simple visual symmetry of the Model, with its twelve 'nodes' and 66 connections, naturally stimulates us to think systemically, develop scenarios, detect patterns, generate $1 + 1 = 3$ creative ideas, understand principles of resilience and sustainability, sense emergent properties of the whole, appreciate the evolution of complex systems over time and the power of small actions to have systemic consequences – all critical competencies for engaging with the contemporary world.

These competencies are stimulated naturally through engagement with the Model. But Hodgson also shows, in the later sections of the book, how the Model can be used intentionally in a variety of settings as a tool for policy, strategy and futures work.

The IFF World Game, which is based on the Model, has already proved immensely popular in many formats – from playful exploration of the future viability of the USA (Case Study 3) through to serious context-setting research for tackling 'wicked' problems like obesity or health inequalities (Case Study 4). Its use in a recent UK Government Foresight project to anticipate the potential impacts on the UK of climate change impacts elsewhere in the world (Case Study 8) begins to show the power for getting to grips with global challenges of a framework that is both truly systemic and simple to grasp. **It offers at last the potential to realise the goal of all resilience thinking: planning for anything without planning for everything.**

That potential is explored in chapters 8 -10 on strategy and policy development and 'creative facilitation to engage the world system'. This is tough, nitty-gritty stuff, based on rich experience – working on difficult problems for clients with little time and failing faith in 'strategy' in a fast-moving world. When Hodgson tells us that the IFF World Game 'enables fast response to changing conditions without sacrificing strategic perspective and power', that 'smart application of the World System Model and World Game will help create strategic resilience' and that the IFF World Game 'is a technique more appropriate to 21st century conditions than scenario planning and conventional strategy analysis' – we would do well to take careful note. He knows of what he speaks.

But this is not a sales pitch for another tool, however effective it may be in practice. Hodgson's intention in developing this work within IFF is to help us address the multiple challenges we face in finding our way to one-planet living. He offers the World System Model as a contribution to growing the capacity in all of us to become more effective global citizens – with a set of capacities, thinking modes, mental models, facilitation and engagement practices that will allow us naturally to think globally and to act wisely with our collective futures in mind. That is the vision for a 'platform for planetary learning' with which the book concludes.

The Club of Rome over 40 years ago identified the 'global problematique' – a series of overlapping and interconnecting planet-level problems. Today we need to be as sophisticated in understanding the complex nature of the 'global resolutique' – the pattern of wise initiatives that will together generate a viable and visionary future for us all. A platform for planetary learning will help us understand the complex nature both of the challenge and of the response, and the need to plan for a learning-based transition between the two.

Lever in hand, Archimedes asked only for a fulcrum and a place to stand in order to move the world. With the World System Model as a basis for designing transformative resilience into our communities and for visioning one-planet living, Hodgson has provided both. Now let's get to work.

Graham Leicester
Director – International Futures Forum

1: Our Global Predicament

Grasping the Whole

We live on a single planet in what has become a massively interconnected world. The impact of our species on the planet now matches the impact of biospheric and atmospheric processes. According to the WWF's *Living Planet Report 2010*[2] survey of planetary indicators:

> *These indicators clearly demonstrate that the unprecedented drive for wealth and well-being of the past 40 years is putting unsustainable pressures on our planet. The Ecological Footprint shows a doubling of our demands on the natural world since the 1960s, while the Living Planet Index tracks a fall of 30 per cent in the health of species that are the foundation of the ecosystem services on which we all depend.*

Another urgent perspective on this comes from research at the Stockholm Resilience Centre. Their Director, Professor Johan Rockström, states:

> *Human pressure on the Earth System has reached a scale where abrupt global environmental change can no longer be excluded. To continue to live and operate safely, humanity has to stay away from critical 'hard-wired' thresholds in [the] Earth's environment, and respect the nature of [the] planet's climatic, geophysical, atmospheric and ecological processes.*[3]

We are already over the planet's limits and the trends are not reversing. This presents us with a threefold challenge:

1) How do we step out of the deeply ingrained, linear way of thinking that divides knowledge and administration into stove pipes of disconnected thought and action?

2) How do we transform our approach to our total human living arrangements so that we become participants in – rather than exploitative liquidators of – the great processes of the Earth and its living system?

3) How do we scale back our impact so that it falls within the real limits of the planetary life-support system – and yet enable a sufficient degree of social justice and meaningful life for all humanity?

These challenges present us with a tangled web of influences and forces. Treating any single factor, such as climate change, in isolation as 'the one big issue', is to make naive assumptions about the cross connections of power in local and global society and ignores the dangers of unintended consequences. The resolution of these challenges requires us to move towards a state of what I and others have called 'one-planet living'.

This book proposes a perspective that can help address this threefold challenge. It argues that we must change the way we think and the way we envision where and how we live, and in what systems of connectedness we are embedded. Otherwise we will continue to seek and apply linear and disconnected solutions to the ever expanding range of problems that we face, thus trapping ourselves in the accelerating downward spiral that turns today's solutions into tomorrow's problems.

That is one step. But we also need to change the way we *think together*. We have gone way past the age of the hero leader. However capable, no individual can match in intelligence the complexity and speed of change that we witness in today's world. For this, we need new ways of developing collective intelligence.

To regain an holistic awareness of the natural systems in which we live we need a framework for visualising and thinking about a deeply interconnected world. The World System Model presented here (Figure 1) is such a framework.

Although based on much research and practical experience in creative thinking, visual thinking, strategy development and scenario planning, the World System Model is essentially a *designed construct*. Like any effective design, it has an aesthetic quality. It enables us to imagine possible futures as well as providing a framework for us to analyse highly interconnected issues. It is designed to be useful on many scales – from planet management to village resilience.

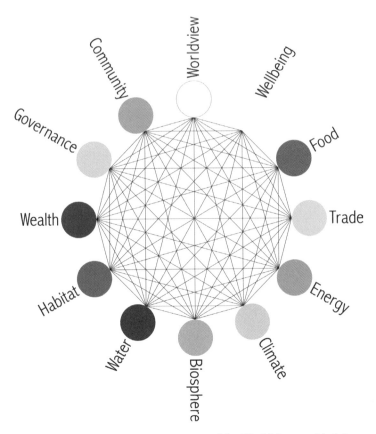

***Figure 1** – The Basic Version of the World System Model*

This World System Model is also the basis for the IFF World Game[4] – a way for groups of people with a common challenge to think through their predicament together in the context of a big picture of the world in which their aspirations can be fulfilled. Combining role play, visual thinking and the democratic methods of the wisdom council, the Game offers an elegant and playful way to generate the kind of information that can stimulate serious results.

As will become clear from the case studies, the Game rapidly induces a sense of collective intelligence in relation to complex issues. The case studies also illustrate IFF's general approach to complex issues in a context of uncertainty: *holism with focus.*

Our Global Challenge

So what is the big picture of the global predicament that the World System Model responds to? Here are a few causes for concern:

- According to the WWF's *Living Planet Report 2010*[5], we were already in 2007 living in a way that consumed the sustainable resources of one and a half planets

- Planetary boundaries research, mentioned above, shows that three of the interlinked planetary boundaries have already been overstepped: climate change, rate of biodiversity loss and changes to the global nitrogen cycle

- *The Millennium Ecosystem Assessment*[6] shows that barely any indicators of environmental health are improving; most are degrading

- Life support systems for all species, not just mankind, are in jeopardy

- The amount of fresh water available to well over half the world's population is diminishing

- The world's oceans are degrading at an accelerating pace, causing massive but little understood species extinction – including the extinction of fish stocks upon which hundreds of millions of people depend

- Even if we were to stop emitting greenhouse gases now, it would still take centuries for the biosphere to restore its natural balance to pre-anthropogenic levels

- Oil production is currently peaking – exacerbating international tension

- The G8 countries are selling over $12 billion per year in arms to the poorest countries. The US spends over $600 billion each year on its military

- 80% of the world's domestic product belongs to 1 billion people; the remaining 20% is shared by about 6 billion people

- 1 in 3 of the world's urban dwellers – more than 900 million people – live in slums, shanty towns, favelas and urban ghettoes

- Three of the largest 'industries' on the planet are armaments, illicit drugs and oil

- Both religious and secular fundamentalism are increasing the world over.

There is no indication that the current trajectory of human activity is changing from the pursuit of growth to the pursuit of steady state economics. That suggests we will lurch even further beyond the carrying capacity of the planet. To respond effectively to this challenge we need to evolve a completely new set of living arrangements that have a footprint commensurate with the planet's actual biocapacity. This, in turn, requires nothing less than a new paradigm for living and a design revolution affecting all aspects of life at all levels of society.

The fragmentation of responsibility, activity and knowledge in society means that issues are rarely perceived – and even more rarely addressed – from the perspective of the overall systems of which they are a part. Efforts, so far, to redress this situation and introduce a more holistic approach backed by systems thinking have been heroic but insufficient given the scale and complexity of the challenge. An obsolete paradigm still dominates, frustrating efforts not only to create the needed breakthroughs but also to implement a great deal of what we already know is needed.

Here are some of that paradigm's conventional wisdoms, which are sustained by denial of our real predicament:

- Economic growth is the *sine qua non* of human success

- Consumption of material goods and entertainment are the two most essential ways of sustaining that growth

- In spite of evidence of the planetary impact of human economic activity, we are still locked into the mistaken belief that pursuit of 'sustainable economic growth' through such policies as the 'low carbon economy' and 'greening the system' will somehow be viable.

From these assumptions we have fashioned a deeply interdependent, 'just in time', globalised trading system that, for all its smart management, is nevertheless brittle in the face of large-scale shocks. We see increasingly frequent examples of this – weather disruption, street protests, erupting volcanoes, terrorist events. All can quickly plunge complex systems into chaos: a dress rehearsal, perhaps, for longer-term collapse.

In IFF we call this *the interrupted society*, highlighting the clear and present danger that large infrastructural breakdowns will paralyse or severely disrupt business as usual. Although we may reassure ourselves that on each occasion we seem to cope and then recover, it is clear that we do not have adequate means to deal swiftly with multiple catastrophes.

Moving Beyond Narrow, Short-Term 'Fixes'

A further difficulty is that the dominant paradigm of governance draws on the rational technological mindset – most notably 'evidence-based policy' – to clarify problems and offer solutions. This involves a combination of economic criteria, scientific analysis (fragmented into specialist disciplines) and technological means.

In this worldview, complexity is supposedly managed by dividing it up into segments of a size to suit the human mind and human organisation. Problems are defined in each segment and analytical thinking is applied to finding the best possible solutions within this limited frame. The assumption is that implementing these segmented solutions will somehow take care of the whole complex and keep the situation under control. This ingrained way of proceeding has served us well for at least 200 years but has now come up against the limitations of its assumptions.

Our world is naturally highly interconnected. It has always been so in its evolution (see, for example, notions of 'the web of life' in wisdom traditions). Our technological world is also unnaturally highly interconnected. By unnatural I mean as a result of human expansion, invention and exploitation. Overlaying these two conflicting forms of interconnectedness means that unexpected behaviour and unintended consequences are bound to emerge; today's solutions become tomorrow's problems; we are faced with episodes of chaotic and non-linear behaviour with which the dominant paradigm is unable to cope.

Our reductionist modes of thinking are increasingly unsuited to what is really going on. IFF calls this a *conceptual emergency*. It is one of the key underlying factors that keep us locked-in to ineffective action.

A second constraint is our fixation on short-term results that can be achieved easily and at relatively low cost. Of course it is important to take action now to bring quick outcomes. For example, we need to produce food and can expand production using fertilisers that depend on fossil oil. But when we look at maintaining the supply of food in the long term we see that the impact of peak oil and rising costs coupled with degradation of the soil could lead to even bigger food shortfalls in the future if we pursue this remedy.

In systems thinking this frequently occurring pattern is called *shifting the burden*. A problem shows itself in the form of a symptom. This provokes the search for a quick solution that, in turn, provides short-term alleviation of the symptom. But, because it is not getting at the root cause, the solution itself builds up a side effect: a further delay in searching for a fundamental solution. The more the short-term relief provided, the longer the resulting procrastination and delay that builds up.

Fundamental solutions, which usually take longer to be effective, have economic and psychological costs that discourage people from applying them and so ensure that the policies chosen and applied are short-term and expedient.

From Fragmentation to Integrity

This would be challenging enough in any one global problem area. But the real challenge is much greater. We are currently applying short-term, sticking plaster remedies in multiple areas, any combination of which could become critical simultaneously.

It is clear then that, before we can initiate and orchestrate an adequate response to our global predicament, we need radically to transform our worldview. We need a much more appropriate and congruent way of looking at, interpreting and participating in the world. We need to develop new capabilities that enable us to act intelligently in what we will call, for ease of reference, *complex messes*. We can recognise a complex mess because:

- It's impossible to agree on one 'correct' view of the situation
- The different reductive views that people have of the problem lead to contradictory solutions

- The many problems caused by the mess are highly interconnected
- Information about the exact nature of the mess is uncertain, with areas of ignorance
- The different values of the actors and stakeholders involved lead to multiple conflicts of interest
- There are clashing ideological, political, cultural and economic constraints
- The consequences of different solutions and scenarios are difficult to imagine
- Vested interests and areas of denial combine to resist change.

Complex messes are often the result of interactions between multiple complex adaptive systems, resulting in the emergence of unpredictable behaviours. They defeat linear, cause-and-effect methods of analysis and response. Indeed such responses frequently make the situation worse by causing unintended consequences. In the new paradigm, entirely new, adaptive *learning methodologie*s are needed. These are explored in detail in Chapters 10 and 11.

The World System Model outlined here aims to provide the platform for a design revolution that harmonises humanity, ecology and technology. It does this by integrating knowledge across disciplines around the major systemic issues confronting our world. The model encourages integrity, marries values with practical effectiveness and can alert us to previously unrecognised interactions, emergent consequences and looming issues. It also provides a platform for deeply informed, pragmatic world visioning.

We can speculate, imagine, even dream better futures. But by 'visioning' I mean something different. Firstly visioning is not simply having a vision but the proactive creation of an image of the future that goes beyond any anticipation. It is a power in the minds of people that calls something new into being. It is seeing a future not as a possibility at some future time, but as an assertion in the present of the way things might be caused to unfold. Visioning is essential because, without it, we are likely to be caught in perpetual loop of trying to fix the old paradigm rather than finding the transformative pathway to one-planet living.

2: The Threat of Synchronous Failure

We are increasingly confronted by major disasters and disruptions that make demands on the emergency services. The most familiar and headline grabbing are natural disasters such as earthquakes and superstorms. Whole swathes of infrastructure can be destroyed in such incidents, affecting millions of people.

Such major events are hard to miss. Less easy to see are the slow changes that gradually build to disruptive proportions. Financial and political crises can be like this. They correspond to what ecologists call *slow variables* that, unrecognised, mount in intensity, reach a threshold and then flip to a crisis state.

Forecasting natural disasters in such a way that people commit resources or change life patterns as a result is difficult. The combination of scientific uncertainty and short-term social pressures compound the problem. So we continue, for example, to build communities on flood plains and cities on geological fault lines.

If this situation were not challenging enough we seem to be entering a period when both natural and man-made disasters and dislocations are increasing in frequency and intensity. This creates a new level of hazard, which has been well characterised by the security analyst Thomas Homer-Dixon as *synchronous failure*.[7]

Living in a world in which multiple major disruptions are likely has implications that have yet to be properly addressed. Despite increasing awareness amongst scientists, governments and the public that we are enmeshed in several types of sustainability issue, the cultural legacy of hundreds of years of administering our affairs through division and department leaves us largely unable to grasp the whole predicament.

The very same characteristics that have made global tele-communications, multinational corporations, globally distributed transportation and a globalised economy so successful are now generating negative results and the potential for global collapse. As we come close to pushing several planetary boundaries beyond their limits and begin to threaten humanity's capacity to survive and thrive in the long term, the criteria that have defined success until now are no longer valid. In fact, we can now begin to see them as measures of ineptitude and failure.

One way to see the range of potential failure zones is to take a comprehensive view of the various dimensions that determine a viable social ecological system. Each of the factors listed below needs to be healthy and sustainable for human society to flourish in its planetary and ecological context.

This list highlights some of the areas where shocks and discontinuities have already occurred or are building up and may well happen. This gives us a basis for considering what challenges synchronous failure might bring:

1. Climate

   Anthropogenic climate change is threatening the planet's life support system

2. Energy

   Escalating energy demand, combined with peak oil, is threatening energy security

3. Water

   Water scarcity and degradation of the world's aquifers are threatening life, food and energy

4. Wealth

   Imbalances and inequalities in material wealth are undermining social stability

5. Governance

   Geopolitically inspired wars revolving around power and resources are making global solutions impossible to implement

6. Food

   The combination of population growth and a largely oil-dependent, rapidly degrading agricultural system is threatening food security

7. Wellbeing

   Psychological stress, unhealthy life styles and a toxic environment are undermining public health

8. Community

   Eroded community coherence and passive dependency within an individualistic and competitive culture are degrading resilience

9. Trade

    The unintended side effects of our flawed version of globalisation are destroying resilient local economies

10. Habitat

    Our habitat (where we live in settlements like villages and cities) and infrastructure (such as water, electricity and transport systems) are ill-suited to rapid change and shock; this means we now live in an increasingly brittle society

11. Biosphere

    Biosphere erosion and the sixth mass extinction, in which 50% of species are disappearing, are unbalancing the ecosystem and reducing the diversity and interrelationships that sustain resilience

12. Worldview

    Fragmented ways of thinking (including the dominance of reductionism and specialisation) and multiple forms of fundamentalism are preventing the emergence of a shared, one-planet living worldview.

An analysis by the UK Government Chief Scientist, John Beddington, is a good example of what might happen if and when just some of these multiple discontinuities converge. He sums this up as a 'perfect storm' of interrelated global events.[8]

As the significance of such synchronous failures emerges in people's minds, it naturally gives rise to increasing anxiety. The habits and beliefs of daily life are contradicted in ways that make meaningful practical responses difficult. The psychologist Maureen O'Hara[9] has characterised three types of response to this growing anxiety. The outcomes for society will be greatly affected by which of these three responses dominates.

The first type of response is essentially neurotic and is characterised by denial. This takes many forms including simplification of the issues, creating 'them' versus 'us' tensions and keeping the boundaries of information tightly controlled. This response also includes clinging to policies that are believed to be solutions when actually they are exacerbating the problem. Such policies include 'sustainable' economic growth, the free market economy and mitigation through regulation. This response may also be reactionary and take the form of repressive social processes aimed at maintaining the existing social order.

The second type of response occurs when the limits of repression of the emerging situation are reached and people can no longer divert and contain the anxiety. The state of anxiety explodes in attempts to annihilate the offending threat even if it means self-destruction. The characteristic state of mind becomes psychotic and chaotic. Violence and depression reduce people's capacity to cope with what is actually happening. This response is a real risk if the third type of response is not cultivated and prepared.

The third type of response is transformational. This occurs when adequate internal and external resources are available to people and they are able to develop new capabilities that increase their resilience as both individuals and communities. The neurotic state, by contrast, tends to be brittle and is likely to crack under strain. The challenge of evoking a transformational response is that the education and life habits that are dominant in both modern and traditional societies do not correspond to this new world demand of one-planet living for an anticipated ten billion people. A transformational response includes the capacity for a creative response to challenge, recognition that collective intelligence is needed and, above all, seeing resilience as a continuous learning and adaptation process. A transformational response generates new, exploratory and positive visions.

One of the first stages of a transformational response is to become aware of how many of today's remedies are either ineffective or counter-productive. Here are some recent examples where propaganda has masked reality:

- The 'war on terror' is actually increasing global insecurity
- Carbon trading isn't reducing greenhouse gas emissions
- The 'green' revolution in agriculture is actually black: dependent on oil
- Corporate social responsibility (CSR) doesn't address the fundamentally dangerous form of an irresponsible, corporate-dominated, legal system
- Continued migration to the cities ignores the limited capacity of those cities to absorb more people.

• Furthermore, political systems based on the nation state, whatever their complexion (left or right, democratic or authoritarian), may not be capable of responding adequately even if the potential for synchronous failure is recognised, since they are all still enmeshed in the old paradigm of prediction, control, competition and manipulation.

In the face of all this, we need to set about creating a new mental, emotional and physical orientation to the world we live in. We need to develop a participative approach and co-create a way of life that transcends dualistic divisions such as 'man-made' vs. 'natural' and aims for appropriate participation in life's process. This will require us to recognise and develop what we might call 21st century capacities to tap in to a different mode of intelligence, both individually and collectively: one that the reductionist mindset doesn't allow for.

This mode of intelligence needs to be able to access multiple ways of seeing and modes of knowledge not restricted to the rationalist view. Decades ago Geoffrey Vickers saw the danger in placing too much reliance on fashionable reductionist models[10]. He anticipated the trend towards relying on abstract models as 'reality'. We have seen this recently in the financial debacles triggered by the misuse of derivatives and 'money as debt' mathematics.

The emerging holistic paradigm that we propose must be better suited to responding to the challenges of a highly interconnected world. There must be honest recognition that we cannot operate in a 'predict, control, compete and manipulate' manner. We lack the necessary understanding and must proceed with humility. Our primary task is action learning, feedback from experiment and holding to the precautionary principle. This approach strengthens resilience. Don Michael put it this way: "What is happening to the human race, in the large, is too complex, too interconnected, and too dynamic to comprehend."[11]

In this participatory worldview, intelligence is freed to harness the latent power in the mind to recognise, visualise and create new patterns and bring about more harmonious conditions. The emphasis is much more that of a designer's mind rather than a scientist's or politician's mind.

Fluency in these 21st century capacities will enable us to subsume our individual creativity in the service of a deeper and broader collective intelligence. When individuals learn to cooperate at a creative level it is possible for the emerging 'group mind' to integrate complexity more effectively than by simply adding separate views or negotiating for the best individual view to win. A genuine synthesis also becomes possible, where the resulting shared insight could not have been arrived at by addition. This level of collective intelligence is often called synergy and is the basis for indigenous people's tradition of the wisdom council.

3: The Opportunity in the Challenge

The severe synchronous challenges discussed in Chapter 2 have the potential to provoke societal collapse. Even before total collapse they might provoke defensive entrenchment within existing power structures and a them-against-us response favouring the wellbeing of some at the expense of others.

These types of response would clearly fall within the psychotic and neurotic categories. So how can we nourish and support the third type of response? How can we prepare our communities and culture so that they are capable of exhibiting a transformational response in the face of converging crises?

A good place to start that inquiry is around the issue of 'resilience', which The Resilience Alliance defines thus:

> *Resilience is... the ability to absorb disturbances, to be changed and then to re-organise and still have the same identity (retain the same basic structure and ways of functioning). It includes the ability to learn from the disturbance. A resilient system is forgiving of external shocks. As resilience declines the magnitude of a shock from which it cannot recover gets smaller and smaller. Resilience shifts attention from purely growth and efficiency to needed recovery and flexibility. Growth and efficiency alone can often lead ecological systems, businesses and societies into fragile rigidities, exposing them to turbulent transformation. Learning, recovery and flexibility open eyes to novelty and new worlds of opportunity.*[12]

Resilience is short-lived unless it is operating in the context of longer term sustainability. So this definition needs to be placed in the context of the conditions for sustainability. Richard Heinberg states five axioms of genuine sustainability:[13]

1) Any society that continues to use critical resources unsustainably will collapse

2) Population growth and/or growth in rates of consumption of resources cannot be sustained

3)   The use of renewable resources must proceed at a rate that is less than or equal to the rate of natural replenishment

4)   The use of non-renewable resources must proceed at a rate that is declining and the rate of decline must be greater than or equal to the rate of depletion

5)   Substances introduced into the environment from human activities must be minimised and rendered harmless to biosphere functions.

We can press the case further still. For, in addition, there is also a psychological, even spiritual, perspective on resilience. The members of a resilient society, while celebrating diversity, will share a vision, an aspiration and a hope. They will inhabit a similar space of meaning and purpose. They will also be constantly working on, and improving, their adaptive capacity. One analogy is with developing the skills for white water canoeing so that the rapids are no longer frightening and fatal.

To generate this kind of resilience, society will need to be highly supportive of collaborative learning in which groups or networks of people practise group problem-solving processes. People will support education that transforms them individually and collectively. Finally a society developing this kind of resilience will organise its affairs from an holistic perspective. It will cultivate ways of knowledge and wisdom that constantly seek to place the part in the whole and seek the meaning in the whole beyond the part.

The customary division into functions that we see in governments and local authorities is very much embedded in the assumptions that underpin a conventional view of resilience. In this dominant model, different requirements (health, transport, infrastructure, social services and so on) are set up as distinct functions and operated largely independently of each other. In a stable environment with few shocks and surprises this kind of separation into 'silos' can work pretty well. When there *are* shocks, the system is supported by a range of emergency services that restore normality as soon as possible.

But we need also to prepare the ground so that we will be ready for synchronous failure, for a cascade of interconnecting shocks to the system: ready for anything. Our current approach is brittle (meaning breaking before bending) and no longer has the flexibility required to accommodate fundamental changes. What is required in order to thrive in the world to come is a new level of adaptive capacity.

The intention behind the World System Model is to prepare the ground for a transformative response. The aim is to support the co-creation of resilient communities and a resilient society, able not only to survive but even to thrive on present and imminent shocks and changes. (In Chapter 12 I describe in more detail the 'transformative resilience' that the World System Model calls for and aims to stimulate.)

The transformative response requires a new interpretation of 'the good life'. Our views and experiences of the good life are usually subconsciously enmeshed in our daily lives so that we are unaware of our assumptions. In *Economics and the Good Life,* Bertrand de Jouvenel describes the task well:

> *The good life, however, is not a product of the market place, but of deliberate and collective decision. It is a task for thoughtful citizens and statesmen, and not simply the sum of millions of separate and amoral 'consumer preferences'.*

Our appreciation of what a good life could be is limited by vested interests such as those of the dominant commercial and political system. This system equates the good life with factors like limitless economic growth, consumption, accumulation of monetary wealth and processed, convenience foods. This means that, when confronted by the need to change these assumptions, people feel aggrieved that they are being required to give up the good life. *What is actually needed is to reframe the essence of the good life in a new system of living.* Evidence is accumulating that moves towards greater resilience actually enhance our experience of the good life. They are not opposing goals if tackled in the right way.

Visioning for one-planet living, which is what we have to do to get 'ready for anything', encapsulates three parallel tasks:

1) We need a creative collective response to the negative challenges in the current situation that could propel us into synchronous failure

2) We need to co-create a viable and equitable way of one-planet living that includes all humanity and the maximum diversity of the biosphere

3) We need a more widespread and better understanding of the possible innovative pathways from here to a viable future.

Underpinning these shifts must be a more systemic and practical framework. The holistic World System Model provides such a framework for considering the range and nature of the fundamental functions of a viable community.

4: An Holistic System Model of the World

The purpose of the World System Model is to provide a framework that better corresponds to the interactive complexity of our social ecological system than the reductionist approach we have become accustomed to. The term 'social ecological system' expresses the view that we can no longer think of humanity as living *in* an ecology but must think of the whole system where society and the way we live is an inseparable part of this wider ecological system. This approach is based on a systems thinking philosophy but the World System Model is not intended to be a model like the system dynamics world model used in the *Limits to Growth*[14] project by the Club of Rome. Rather, the World System Model is a simple framework to help envision how human ecosystems on any scale need to hold together a minimum set of twelve key factors and allow them to interrelate.

From a systems thinking perspective, an objective model of the world is impossible. All we can do is to work towards a progressive approximation that takes into account a chosen perspective. However, if our implicit mental models contradict our chosen perspective, then they will be at best ineffective and at worst seriously misleading. The notion of sustainability has suffered this fate because the ideal is at odds with a mental model that requires sustained economic growth. At the same time, the modest changes we are making are our not keeping pace with the accelerating risks.[15]

Since the perspective we are taking in this book is grounded in whole systems, and aims to be alert to complex interconnections, we need matching mental models upon which we can base policy, decisions and life-style choices. We have entered a period where our views of the world we live in (whether they are 'modern' or 'traditional') are increasingly incongruent with what that world actually is and how it is responding to us. The result is all kinds of misconstrued and unintended consequences that are destroying the possibility of a good life, for us humans and for the living Earth.

The basic structure of the World System Model (see Figure 1 in Chapter 1) comprises a set of twelve interacting factors that are called nodes. There could, of course, be many more than twelve nodes. Yet the choice of these twelve is not arbitrary. They offer a pretty comprehensive, top-level, summary assessment of the viability of any social ecological system.

The value for the total system of any particular node is best understood by posing a question: can a society be viable if any one of these nodes is weak or absent? Overall, the nodes cover a range of dimensions that ensure the World System Model is a *social ecological system* rather than being just social or just ecological. The terms used are designed to be close to the basic necessities of a balanced life and are simple enough that the same pattern can be used with experts and children and all those in between. It can also operate at many levels of recursion (for example villages, cities, bioregions, countries, continents and the whole planet). The system is arranged in a way that has mnemonic power (it resembles a clock face) and, finally, the nodes have been formulated to encourage interdisciplinary interaction rather than expert silos.

The diagram of the World System Model:

- Provides a framework for holding in mind twelve key factors referred to as *nodes*

- Shows the multiple connections between the nodes and thus represents – and aids recognition of – the interactive complexity of the social ecological system

- Colour codes each node to emphasise that each node is different in character and plays a different role in the whole system

- Uses the circle as a symbol of wholeness and to indicate that every node in the system has equal value – the system is not a hierarchy

- Implies that anything happening anywhere in the system is likely to have a knock-on effect in other parts of the system.

Each of the twelve nodes of the World System Model is considered an essential component of a viable or sustainable human society and each node is connected to every other node so the whole diagram presents a network of connections inside the circle.

Between the twelve nodes there are 66 binary connections. Changes in a single node are referred to as first order. Changes occurring through interaction of nodes are called second order effects. Powerful systemic couplings across several nodes are called third order effects.

The main points to bear in mind when reading the diagram are:

- The World System Model is a set of twelve interdependent, mutually relevant **factors**, each indicating a component or node in the system essential for viable human life in the context of the planet.

- The **interconnections** mean that a change of state in any given factor may trigger, induce or otherwise modify a change of state in another factor.

- Each factor has a **condition** which is the state of health or viability at the current time.

- This condition is not static, but is changing and thus reveals a **trend** or direction of change.

- The direction of change may be towards *increased* viability or *decreased* viability.

- A trend may accelerate or change direction such that it becomes a **discontinuity** which generates a shock or surprise This could be positive or negative in relation to viability. Common terms for discontinuities are 'trend-break', 'tipping point', 'peak' and 'runaway condition'.

- Discontinuities in a given factor often have greater cross impact on other factors and can create a **domino effect** in which the effects spread throughout the system causing multiple parallel discontinuities. There are instances where improvement in one node viewed in isolation creates problems in other nodes if there are not synchronous adjustments.

- It is possible that multiple discontinuities may occur without interaction or direct causal connection. This can lead to **synchronous failure** or **synchronous success** in terms of overall world viability. In everyday speech these may be referred to as either unfortunate or happy coincidences.

The initial use of this World System Model framework is for scanning. It provides a way of organising information on first order trends and discontinuities. A version of such a database has been developed on the IFF website[16]. The World System Model acts as an organising portal which enables the reader to explore the trends, discontinuities and information sources for each of the nodes.

The model can also be used to map interconnectedness. This is essentially about representing linkages in the world system in such a way that a change in one end of the link leads to a change in the other. In this sense, there is some similarity with the arrows used in causal loop diagramming. However, the focus here is not on feedback loop dynamics as such but rather on the implication that focusing on isolated effects and dealing with one node at a time will lead us to fall into the trap – or missed opportunity – of overlooking knock-on effects.

These linkage effects can be negative or positive. In the case of synchronous failure or 'perfect storms' we are interested in the negative synchronisation of the links. However, the other great value of connectedness mapping is the *search for synchronous success*. In this form, an action in one node increases the health of other nodes and so we get more effect or results from a given intervention or investment.

Working with the model also acts as a kind of cognitive gymnasium. It is not only a framework for organising information. In practice it actually helps develop cognitive skills that are more conducive to holistic thinking. In this respect it is functioning in roughly the same way as a mandala in other traditions – providing a way to hold a lot of complex information in mind at the same time.

Another factor is speed: the model helps us reach insights faster. Analytic methods, especially where large amounts of data are involved, take a long time to assimilate. Logical analytical structures help but they tend to be algorithmic and still sequential and time consuming. This model is designed to support the human capacity for *patterned thinking,* which grasps situations in an holistic or big picture way.

Understanding based on pattern recognition is much more rapid than analysis – a key factor in a rapidly changing world. The visual representation of the World System Model thus offers a completely different way of tackling difficult and complex challenges.

Another important feature is scale-linking. The system model can be applied at many scales from village to country to whole planet. It is what systems thinkers call recursive; that is to say, the same pattern repeats itself at different scales. Viable planets need viable countries, which need viable cities in their turn.

In this way, data scanning in different communities can be understood at a larger scale by local administrations. Their own data scanning can, in turn, be understood by national administrations. The same applies for policy and action at each level: using the World System Model, political leadership should become holistic and integrated.

The implications of applying the model in practice in policy and strategic decision-making is explored further, with examples, in Chapters 7 and 8. Its potential for contributing to the way we learn to become active, engaged, informed global citizens is developed much further in Chapter 11, which also elaborates on the potential of the World System Model as a platform for planetary learning.

5: The Twelve Nodes

What follows is a summary of the meaning of the twelve nodes of the World System Model. A more complete description, including threatening discontinuities, appears on the IFF website.

1. Wellbeing

The Wellbeing node includes: Population health, Sense of security, Addictive behaviour, Degree of happiness, Self-responsibility, Creative expression, Perceived and actual quality of life.

There is an increasing risk of non-linear changes in the ecosystems that support human life, including accelerating, abrupt and potentially irreversible changes. Similar non-linearities are anticipated in socio-economic and political contexts. For example, widespread food insecurity resulting from severe climate change, institutional failure and increasingly damaged soils could worsen inequality and lead to conflict. At the same time, a great many individually less dramatic losses in 'ecosystem services' are likely to influence human health adversely.

2. Food

The Food node includes: Agriculture and horticulture, Food quality, Nutritional balance, Food safety, Equitable distribution.

So-called 'green revolution' technologies have supported the massive growth in world population. They include pesticides, herbicides, synthetic nitrogen fertiliser (mostly developed from fossil fuels), irrigation projects and higher-yield crop varieties.

Although yields have been much higher than in traditional agricultural systems, this has not taken into account the amount of land that was cleared or irrigated for the green revolution. The latest statistics show a major drop in the productivity of land that has been intensively farmed for the past 30 years due to desertification and other forms of land degradation. This process has also seen the industrialisation of food production and a shift from subsistence-oriented cropland towards producing grain with high virtual water content for export and for animal feed.

3. Trade

The Trade node includes: Transport of goods, Mobility of people, Free/fair trade, Markets and agreements, Regional economies, Trade support systems.

Trade is the age-old process of exchange between people, businesses and nations. Although global trade has a long history, there are some characteristics that arise from our 'shrinking planet' that make its impact greater than ever before. The power provided by fossil fuels and engine technology, combined with containerisation, has created a shipping industry that can transport bulk materials around the world relatively rapidly. This has enabled China, for example, to become a manufacturing centre for the world. Air transport has speeded up exchange of smaller packages including food, and all this is logistically supported by global digital communications and computing. Software itself is a widely traded commodity. The transfer of funds and other financial instruments is now virtually instant and global. In the era of cheap oil and developed infrastructure, we have created a just-in-time, make-anything-anywhere, global trade system which is extremely brittle in its vulnerability to disruption.

4. Energy

The Energy node includes: Fossil sources, Renewable sources, Nuclear resources, Energy intensity and efficiency, Distribution and application, Energy security.

Humans live in and from the biosphere. But in the first decade of the 21st century, 85% of the primary energy consumed by the population of 6.7 billion humans comes from the lithosphere – below ground. About 40% of this energy is oil, another 40% comes from natural gas and coal, and 6% is from uranium. Very little of it is renewable, and all of it releases elements into the atmosphere that affect the global climate. Energy has become the overarching resource and dependency question of our globalising, commercial-industrial civilisation (although many argue that water will soon become the most pressing issue in this regard). Our current patterns of use and dependency were set in the industrial revolution based on abundant coal and the subsequent exponential growth in the availability of cheap oil. The use of energy varies from region to region, climate to climate and industry to industry. However, the main dependencies on plentiful fossil fuel are now deeply ingrained in both local and global systems. The most demanding are heating/cooling of buildings, agriculture, transport and electricity generation.

5. Climate

The Climate node includes: Weather patterns, Greenhouse gas emissions, Temperature rise, Ice melt and sea level, Mitigation activity.

Global warming is occurring – there is a growing body of observations of increasing air and ocean temperatures, widespread melting of snow and ice, and rising sea levels. Since the beginning of the industrial revolution the burning of fossil fuels, land use change and agricultural practices have significantly increased the atmospheric concentrations of greenhouse gases such as carbon dioxide (CO_2), methane (CH_4) and nitrous oxide (N_2O). Scientific research and knowledge on climate change have also progressed substantially, confirming that the current acceleration of warming of the Earth's climate is almost certainly due in large part to these human activities. The effects of warming are not fully understood but increasing superstorms, reversals of El Niño in the southern ocean, extreme rainfall with flooding, and desertification of previously fertile regions are part of already existing and intensifying trends.

6. Biosphere

The Biosphere node includes: State of organic life, Species extinction, Wilderness, Forms of pollution, Exploitation and degradation, Conservation and restoration.

Humanity, while buffered against (and blinded to) some environmental immediacies by culture and technology, is fully dependent on the flow of services provided by the interconnected ecosystems that make up the biosphere. The *Millennium Ecosystem Assessment* Reports[17] (a key source for information on the state of the biosphere) define four categories of ecological service on which we entirely depend to sustain human life: *supporting services* such as soil and oxygen formation, nutrient cycling and primary production; *provisioning services* like food, fibres and fresh water; *regulating services* that keep climate, air and water quality, as well as human and animal diseases, regulated in a way that enables life as we know it. Fourthly, we benefit non-materially from ecosystems through spiritual enrichment, cognitive development, reflection and recreation.

7. Water

The Water node includes: Rainfall and ice-melt patterns, The state of aquifers, rivers and lakes, Irrigation and industrial demands, Purity and distribution, Scarcity and contamination.

Although they hold less than 0.5% of the Earth's total freshwater, surface waters, including lakes, ponds, reservoirs, rivers, streams and wetlands represent 80% of the renewable surface water available in a given year. Loss and degradation of inland water habitats is widespread; it is estimated, for example, that by 1985 56-65% of suitable inland water systems had been drained for agriculture in Europe and North America. These water bodies provide a wide range of ecosystem services from drinking water, energy and recreation, to irrigation and transport, but the capacity of inland water systems to provide these services is in decline. Water pollution is widespread in many countries – reducing the capacity of inland waters to filter and assimilate waste, as well as having direct impacts on biodiversity. The huge majority of the Earth's unfrozen freshwater is found below the surface in aquifers as groundwater. Groundwater is theoretically renewable as long as it is not withdrawn faster than nature can replenish it, but in many dry regions it does not renew itself, or only very slowly, and intensive pumping is withdrawing it at unsustainable rates. Few countries measure the quality of groundwater or the rate at which it is being exploited. This makes the severity of the problems difficult to assess and to manage.

8. Habitat

The Habitat node includes: Settlements on all scales, Infrastructure and utilities, Design quality, Degradation and restoration, Urban ecological footprints, Work life relationships.

In 1950 there were 86 cities in the world with a population over one million; today there are 400, and by 2015 there will be at least 550. Cities have absorbed nearly two-thirds of the global population explosion since 1950 and are currently growing by a million babies and migrants each week. The present urban population (3.2 billion) is larger than the total population of the world in 1960. The global countryside, meanwhile, has reached its maximum population (3.2 billion) and will begin to shrink after 2020. As a result cities will account for *all* future world population growth from that point on - expected to peak at about 10 billion in 2050. The infrastructure upon which they depend is vulnerable to a range of natural and climate disasters as well as to degradation through shortage of capital for maintenance and reconstruction.

9. Wealth

The Wealth node includes: Finance and economy, Values and lifestyle, Work and reward, Equity and distribution, Monetary systems, Freedom and regulation.

Wealth here represents a viable lifestyle, able to provide in substance (not just in dollars per day) a decent human life while allowing a future for subsequent generations. Finance and monetary wealth are partial and often misleading indicators of real wealth. The most prevalent measures of wealth like GDP (gross domestic product) are quite inadequate. For example, the economic activities of cleaning up pollution, destroying the forests, over-fishing the seas and engaging in destructive warfare are all included in GDP, as is the money generated by the enterprises that produce these damaging effects. This is mainly because our current economic system is underpinned by the necessity of growth which is clearly unsustainable.

10. Governance

The Governance node includes: Political systems, Civic participation, Local, national and international policies, Regulation and subsidies, Exploitation, Corruption and oversight, Public order, Propaganda and terrorism.

Governance is probably the most intractable issue on the planet – given its role in addressing the challenges and interconnections in all other areas. Governance is not government. It is a process: the process by which institutions, organisations, corporations, societies and other actors 'guide' themselves. It is also about how these bodies interact with each other and with their stakeholders. At its most basic level it is about how society organises itself for collective decision-making. We live in a world of complexity, uncertainty and rapid change, in which national governments are increasingly powerless to act alone. Governance today requires certain leadership capacities that are poorly developed even in the most powerful nations and cities. They include an ability to take decisions without clear evidence in situations of inherent uncertainty; a tolerance of ambiguity combined with a capacity for rapid learning; the ability to take people along with you while fully acknowledging uncertainty; and a new capability for thinking through critical decisions in an holistic way that is able to handle multiple possible scenarios. At an even more fundamental level, the connected world raises questions about the boundaries of community and, therefore, of representation, that go to the heart of defining democracy.

11. Community

The Community node includes: Living arrangements, Life span education, Civic capacity, Social capital, Competition and mutuality, Resilience, Identity and Belonging.

Community in the World System Model essentially encompasses the different ways people live together with some degree of mutual interdependence. The word community is used rather than society because, in seeking to understand the interactions of the eleven other factors with groups of people, it is communities that increasingly determine reaction and response. Communities may bring together a number of elements, such as solidarity, commitment, mutuality and trust, or they may have a particular focus. For example: communities of location, virtual communities, communities of practice, communities of culture (including communities of need or identity: e.g. ethnic or religious groups, people with disabilities, frail or aged people, etc.) and community organisations. Community may in general be positive in terms of mutual support, but it can also be insular, exclusive and intolerant. Community is also used to cover the intergenerational aspects of society, especially education. Particularly relevant at the moment is the extent to which communities are resilient, that is to say how well they are able to bounce back after shocks and even disasters.

12. Worldview

The Worldview node includes: Dominant belief systems, Tolerance and fundamentalism, Values and outlooks, Ideologies and utopias, Fixed or dynamic attitudes, Mental models, The place of consciousness.

Worldview refers to the way human beings visualise themselves as part of society, of nature and of the cosmos. These views are largely unconscious but are questioned in times of crisis and by those endowed with a greater inclination towards conscious inquiry. The practical consequence of a worldview is that it determines our values and actions. If our actions are failing but our worldview prevents us from seeing that is what is happening, we have a crisis that cannot be averted. Our attempts at remediation will just be 'more of the same'. Equally, if we can consciously cultivate a worldview more appropriately responsive to the reality of our situation, our actions are more likely to be successful and enable us to learn. In the face of the unknown and of converging crises, many people tend to cling to – and further rigidify – their existing worldviews, which prevents precisely what is needed for a transformative response: an increased ability to learn, be flexible and respond creatively and appropriately. The systems thinker Fritjof Capra suggested in the early 1990s that the growing and converging social, ecological, and economic crises have one and the same root cause: a 'crisis of perception', or in other words a crisis of consciousness based on a culturally dominant form of thinking and meaning-making that is no longer appropriate.

.

6: From World System Model to World Game

The World System Model establishes an holistic structure for visioning the state of the world and, thereby, a platform for understanding our global predicament, assessing innovations and designing wise initiatives. So how can it be usefully employed in such a way?

We have found the model very useful as a technical tool in a number of situations including, for example, research and policy-making. However, there is often some resistance to the model's apparent complexity and the daunting range of material it embraces. This response can slow learning and assimilation and can reduce the intended benefits.

We have found the most effective way to overcome this challenge has been to introduce the World System Model to groups, teams and communities of people in the form of a game – the IFF World Game.

The IFF World Game engages people immediately. It uses the World System Model as a gameboard and has people role-playing and tackling real-world case studies in a way that simulates the integral management of complexity. As a game, it engages the emotions and perceptions as well as thinking. We can 'game' our way into complexity even if we cannot analyse our way in.

The 'gaming' character is more apparent in the overall approach to the complex subject matter rather than in any element of competition. The main characteristic of the Game is that it is designed for collaborative learning: the competition is not between people but between the group and the world challenges that the group faces.

Playing the Game also helps to develop and access a collective intelligence amongst a group of people who share a common challenge. In organisational learning theory this is called the development of a shared mental model (which is perhaps the best sense in which the World System Model is a 'model').

Collective intelligence goes further than this in that it is possible also to cultivate shared wisdom. Wisdom is the basis of sound judgement and, where a group of people needs to share a concerted judgement, the creation of a common appreciative system is essential. Working with the World System Model in a facilitated environment or in the gaming context speeds up the generation of collective wisdom. By role-playing a wider range of responsibilities in the World Game, people become better equipped to take responsibility as global citizens, whatever scale of involvement they have. The World System Model and its associated games become a key contribution to education for one-planet living.

The core structure of the World Game is the diagram of twelve nodes shown in Figure 1. In each of the twelve nodes, as we have seen, there are major trends and potential disruptions that could have an impact on any of our future plans at any scale. The World Game provides a structure in which to explore those possibilities rather than shy away from them. Some versions of the Game can also deliberately feed the creative impulse by including promising developments and innovations as part of the context around each node.

Without some insight into the pattern of interconnections between these areas and possible synchronous failures, seemingly reasonable actions in one area may create unintended consequences in others. The Game builds up an holistic perspective that is shared by all the players and intended to guard against this happening.

The World Game works on any scale, from a family to a community, from a city or country to the whole planet. It can be both the basis for asking deeply practical questions about concrete local realities, and for exploring people's beliefs about future planetary viability and what we need to lead a good life.

In the most common version of the Game each node is allocated to an individual or a team: they take responsibility for that node (and whatever the world might 'throw at it') whilst addressing a specific issue. Together the twelve players or teams might form a 'world government' or a specialist commission or a city council – depending on the focus of the Game.

The twelve players quickly inform themselves about their specific node area – the global trends and possible discontinuities that need to be considered. They then come to a judgement about which are most relevant or most concerning given the issues under discussion. This first phase of the Game thus provides a new map of the future landscape that needs to be traversed.

The next phase looks at interconnections in the World System Model. Players explore connections and future consequences with other areas – a form of rapid global scenario generation. In some games random 'wild card' events are thrown into the mix at this point. Where players first immersed themselves in engaging with a single node, this second phase has them lose themselves more deeply in the complexity of the interconnected world.

The Game process culminates in a 'wisdom council' in which each player voices their perspective on the issue at hand in light of their learning experience and their new, more holistic understanding of the interconnected global operating environment. Players speak from this perspective to suggest 'far-sighted actions' that might avoid impending disaster, capitalise on opportunity or allow for swifter recovery in the event that bad things happen.

One of the key elements of playing the World Game is talking. The richness and meaning of the World System Model is extended through players' discussions, their engagement with the nodal briefs provided to them, their willingness to consider the connections between the various nodes of the World System Model and the shared creation of the narratives formed while playing the Game. This all helps develop a collective intelligence in the group.

A second crucial feature of the World Game is its emphasis on a playful approach, giving players permission to approach concepts and challenges that might otherwise be either daunting and difficult to engage with or not an official part of their usual work. This seems to be a vital feature in promoting the kinds of discussion that the Game facilitates best. Nothing is excluded or off the table.

Naturally there are those who question whether this is really a 'game' in the technical sense. The process possesses an underlying systemic structure, but it does not contain many examples of the sort of codified and systematised interactions between players that might be thought of as 'game mechanics'. There is no 'win condition' in the World Game, no way to out-compete fellow players or to best the system itself.

Success in the Game comes from a team of players pitting themselves against the challenges of a complex, interacting world. It is a playful engagement with the concepts represented by the World System Model. Emphasising this aspect of the activity, its open-ended and generative nature is preserved and recognised. Put another way, *the competitive element is transferred from a battle between individuals to a struggle of the collective to transform the world situation.* The very nature of the complex challenge demands collaboration for success.

The World Game is evolving in three ways:

1)   'Game in a box' which is self-moderated (including in a simple downloadable version)[18]

2)   Face-to-face, role-play group game with facilitator (as described above)

3)   Web-based version which enables remote interaction.

Our intention is that the 'game in a box' version will very quickly make this simple tool available to large numbers of people. The facilitated, workshop-based group version of the World Game is already proving its worth as a rapid engagement tool for groups seeking to take wiser decisions in the face of an uncertain future. The web-based collaborative game would require considerable work, in order for a computational interaction between variables to be assessed and a conclusion reached. Such a game would have interesting possibilities in conjunction with a platform for planetary learning (see Chapter 11).

In summary, the IFF World Game is a conceptual framework for rapidly appraising the context of viable societies on any scale from village to planet, anticipating and actively engaging with whatever might lie ahead, and generating, by collective intelligence, far-sighted actions to increase viability and resilience.

The IFF World Game is an energising way for groups of people to increase their awareness and understanding of the issue of the resilience needed for sustainability as a pattern of interconnected factors. It provides a comprehensive basis for collaborative projects in sustainability and resilience-building at multiple scales (local, regional, national, global). It is an enjoyable education in whole systems thinking that does not need any technical background.

As people in communities and organisations realise that they are challenged by a complex of interacting factors in the global situation and that their local solutions are vulnerable to these wider factors, they need to prepare effectively. Since this is at first glance both a complex and a scary situation, it greatly helps for people to become alerted to it in the form of a game. In this format people can absorb the implications of our global predicament in a playful way that does not shut down their creativity with worry and confusion.

The World Game is relevant for anyone interested in the current world situation and its implications for local life. It is especially good for groups who want to improve their capacity for shared problem-solving and the co-creation of activities to help them achieve their goals for a better society.

Figure 2 *– A Wisdom Council in a World Game session, mapping and discussing interconnections (represented by ropes laid between the node positions)*

So far the Game has proven very useful to community groups, organisations developing strategy, policy-makers needing to look at the big picture some way into the future, and decision-makers who have responsibility for sustainability in all its forms. Case examples of diverse IFF World Game applications appear at various points in the rest of this book. The next three chapters examine in more detail the application of the Game in a variety of settings – starting with communities, moving on to the public sector and local government and concluding in Chapter 9 with the World Game applied to a whole country.

Ultimately, playing the IFF World Game should be a worthwhile learning experience for anyone who claims to be a global citizen. One day we hope the Game will be an accepted part of the global educational system: a way of learning about the World System Model. The speed at which the Game has been taken up by the groups and organisations that have so far been introduced to it suggests that its use will spread rapidly over the coming years, especially as it becomes available online.

7: Using the World Game to Help Communities Improve Resilience

Global problems, even in their local manifestation, require transdisciplinary thinking integrating different disciplines. This approach is emerging more strongly as people increasingly identify multiple interacting problems in different fields.[19] This can prove difficult and time-consuming without a unifying framework. The most important implications of any problem tend to reside in the often-overlooked and little-understood interstices between better-known and measurable factors. Design and decision-making based on the whole system and its interconnections – what Buckminster Fuller called the 'pattern integrity' – is much more likely to result in actions that foster sustainability and resilience. Experts or people with experience who frame their discussions in this way will tend to make more rapid progress in both mutual understanding and generating solution ideas.

Intentional Communities

The IFF World Game can help players learn about world affairs at a practical level, especially the nature of interdependency and the consequences of ignoring or overlooking it. There is much curriculum material around already, of course. The World System Model offers a complementary tool that helps to integrate and relate this information and acts as a frame for holistic overview and interpretation.

It is challenging to engage with the degree of complexity and interconnectivity that makes up what has been called the "world problematique", let alone understand what can be done to address it. The World System Model provides a symbolic framework by creating a form that holds all of that complexity and inter-relationship for the players of the World Game. As noted earlier, like a mandala, it has a carrying power that enables us to 'rest' a complicated and unstable set of concepts, feelings and relationships in a visual picture. That picture can then work in different ways – cognitive, informational, psychological – and can, where needed, come to carry a ritual significance. For example, the value of wisdom council processes is the way they help the people involved to develop a sense of shared meaning that also strengthens their capacity for concerted action.

The World Game gives permission to be playful and imaginative and to have some fun with the people with whom we share our predicament. It allows room for everything from gallows humour to inspiring personal experience to getting tangled up in the web of interconnections. The adaptability of the basic format means that it can be tailored to suit the mood, intention or capacity of the group playing it.

Playing together develops a collective insight into current challenges by enabling players to tap into their collective intelligence. Through a process of social interaction and learning it helps people move beyond their individual cognitive bias while challenging the received 'groupthink' and cultural stories that dominate our current understanding.

Since the World Game works on any scale, it is a practical tool for engaging directly with axioms like "think global act local" and "be the change you want to see in the world", and enables us to contextualise our ideas and actions in meaningful ways. It can be both the basis for asking practical questions about concrete local realities, and for exploring philosophical ideas about what we need to lead a good life.

An inherent focus on relationship and interconnectivity is embedded at every level, building our capacity to think and feel and ask questions that engage with multiple issues systemically. This can be as simple as recognising the connection between growing food, needing to water it, and getting the energy to pump the water – all the way through to more complicated interconnections exploring feedback loops and unintended consequences, for example, of different governance processes as distinct from policy content.

Essentially the power of playing the World Game as a group with a facilitator is that we can begin to tell ourselves and each other different stories, in which the power of intent and vision and the willingness to explore what it is we truly value, reconnects us to one another and to our fragile world.

Playing the Game doesn't bring answers that will 'save the world', for life is too complicated and subtle for that, but it can enable us to stay, collectively, with difficult questions, which brings a healing of its own. From here we can spin new stories of what the good life on a sustainable planet might look like and begin, step by step, to act our way into them.

Playing the Game alerts us to the challenges we face in a constructive way, helps us to anticipate and be ready for change and, with follow-on collaboration, improves our resilience and capacity to bounce back after shocks and surprises. Its most creative application is as a platform for the design of new community living arrangements that are consistent with long-term harmony with the living planet.

~Case Study 1~

Community Game: Findhorn Foundation, Scotland

A day-long workshop was held with representatives of the Findhorn Community, including the Findhorn Foundation, the Findhorn College, and the New Findhorn Association. The workshop took the form of playing the IFF World Game. The first phase involved the gaming scenario of participants being asked to research and report back to the mayor of a medium-sized city on the core challenge: *"What might be the biggest challenges to our city's resilience in the next ten years?"*

Participants were asked to research the global situation, trends and possible discontinuities while focusing on the twelve factors of the World System Model. The aim was to identify a key concern for each of the twelve factors. The second phase was a 'fast and frugal' round of scenario exercises to consider the interactions of some of these global trends and discontinuities, including their potential impact on the hypothetical city in the event of synchronous failure or disruption in a number of areas.

The third phase brought the results of the Game closer to the real world of the Findhorn Community by assuming that the fictional mayor had asked the members of the community what Findhorn could do to help his city in particular and to avoid catastrophic scenarios in general. The lessons and insights from the day were synthesised through a 'wisdom council' that resulted in a list of declaration statements about how to address the most pressing issues faced by communities.

Participant Feedback

"...synergistic in conception, practice and result. Pacing was perfect for me. Experience a next step in self-awareness and relationship to the whole."

"Inspiring and concrete, thank you for a new useful tool. Would be interested in getting training for this kind of session."

"Useful to put it ALL out in one go... i.e. see so many issues and their synergy at once."

~Case Study 2~

City Game: Dundee, Scotland
(Sponsored by the RSA)
Participants had responded to the following challenge:

As concerned citizens, you are invited to explore possible futures for Dundee City using the framework of the World System Model developed by IFF. This will lead you to review critical global trends and potential discontinuities and disruptions that are likely to affect the future of Dundee. The method for engaging with this exploration is through a game. The World System Model becomes a 'game board' on which you will role play in an intense but light-hearted way an *advisory council to Dundee City*. The game is very permissive to creative thinking: whatever we think and say 'it's only a game'. However, useful, even exciting insights are generated that inform serious considerations. We hope the conversation will generate some serious insights about the future of the city.

Participant Feedback
"It is remarkable how much ground has been covered in such a short time, and how quickly we have 'got on to the same page'."

"The IFF World Game process could be very effective in generating ideas for social innovations and social enterprise."

~Case Study 3~

Nation Game: San Francisco, USA
Hosted by International Futures Forum

The subject chosen for the purposes of introducing the game and having an enjoyable and relevant conversation in San Francisco was: *the future viability of the US over the next 20 years.*

Volunteers were first appointed to twelve Cabinet Secretary posts corresponding to the twelve nodes of the World System Model. Together with a number of special advisers they collectively formed the US Government for the afternoon.

In the middle phase of the game four groups each took on imagining possible impact scenarios if a combination of three major shocks happened simultaneously – the idea of synchronous failures.

Scenario A: Climate plus Wealth plus Habitat Crisis
Headlines:
Largest population shift in US history
Industrial agriculture fails
Rebirth of small-scale, artisan economies

Scenario B: Food plus Trade plus Community Crisis
Headlines:
Saudi Arabia shuts off oil supplies
Farms guarded by militia and the rich hoard food
Massive reduction in fresh food availability

Scenario C: Water plus Energy plus Governance Crisis
Headlines:
Prevalence of famine and disease
Currency collapse and food riots
Resource-rich communities protecting themselves
Collapse of community collaboration

Scenario D: Wellbeing plus Biosphere plus Worldview Crisis
Headlines:
Mankind temporarily outsmarts nature until monoculture solution fails
Drought leading to food and energy failure
Suicide and crime epidemics

In the final phase a Wisdom Council was called to generate ideas to head off or survive the crises with far-sighted actions. A range of policy ideas was called forth:

Wellbeing: Train all leaders in consciousness, transformation, new leadership skills. Let consciousness rule.
Nurture all positive solutions designed from a basis of trust (global, not just the US).

Food: Link production and consumption levels for planetary sustainability.
Food is a necessity. Protect purity and sanctity of natural resources.

Trade: Lead in establishing global goal of shared, sustainable prosperity. Global governance to match this.
Empower people and communities to produce food locally.

Energy: Address our fears: regular fireside chats about transformative resilience.

Climate: Run down the carbon economy, reinvest in local community and green technology.

Rapid move from fossil fuels. Move from the coast. Save water and prepare for system collapse.

Biosphere: Make long-term consequences more visible.

Understand threat to environment. Defer to scientific warnings and evidence.

Water: Conserve supply, reduce use and contamination. Reduce demand through taxation.

Build green energy grid. Conserve energy and water.

Habitat: Prepare people for inevitable losses we must face. Human love is an infinite resource. Hope not fear.

Support capacity to live sustainably – with community building, systemic understanding and investment.

Wealth: Create conditions for locally sustainable equitable economies.

Reframe 'wealth' and 'success' to redefine the American Dream.

Governance: Provide leaders with safety and spaces to think.

Bring humanity and compassion to work – full human potential.

Provide appropriate information openly and freely to government and governed.

Community: Economic justice as the marrow of all social policy and innovation.

Shake hands with, and respect, communities of the world.

Let the rich know the poor.

Worldview: Build capacity for logical reasoning *and* love.

Recognise labours of others across the world. Failure of one is failure of all.

Participant Feedback

"The game provided an easy entry to complexity."

"There is an elegance about the game that stimulates creativity because of its constraints."

"It is game like in giving us permission to get beyond our normal assumptions."

"Play wakes up our capacity for problem solving. Always has done."

21ˢᵗ Century Hopscotch: World Gaming in the Playground

If understanding of the global situation is increasingly going to be important to global citizens then it is vital to be able to share world visioning in community and family settings. Variations of the IFF World Game have been played in intergenerational settings. These are firmly based on cultivating face-to-face relationships through embodied physical learning, emphasising the social nature of the game.

One particularly invigorating version of the game to be played with small children has the underlying game board converted to a playground format with large coloured circles that players can stand on in order to experience different kinds of physical and mental action.

To make the IFF World Game intelligible and accessible to a younger age range, as well as suitable for family participation, modifications were made in the language used to describe the nodes. For example:

Worldview	becomes	Beliefs, Understanding
Wellbeing	becomes	Happiness, Health
Food	remains	Food
Trade	becomes	Trading
Energy	becomes	Fuel, Electricity
Climate	becomes	Climate, Weather
Biosphere	becomes	Nature
Water	remains	Water
Habitat	becomes	Buildings and streets
Wealth	becomes	Money
Governance	becomes	Leaders
Community	becomes	Family & Friends

This form of the game is initiated by a treasure hunt based around the twelve nodes and an art activity based around connections between the nodes. Playground games also go through three phases: familiarising players with the names of the nodes, making connections between nodes, and telling stories around connections. Our experience is that parents and other adults very willingly join in to support the children with the main game and the ancillary activities.

The treasure hunt is a fun way of getting to know the nodes, as well as giving the facilitators a way of gathering some evidence of participants' responses to the nodes. Participants in the treasure hunt have to find the twelve pieces of the World Game hidden around the play area. In a World Game played with children from the Calthorpe community in East London, UK the 'treasure' took the form of a helium balloon in the appropriate node colour attached to a brief description with some prompting questions and a symbol representing the node. Once a node had been found, the symbol had to be copied onto the participant's 'treasure hunt pack'. Participants were then invited to respond with any thoughts or feelings about the node by attaching a tag to the balloon. Once they had collected all twelve symbols, players came to collect their prize. The treasure hunt is also a useful way to fill/decorate the space. Because it is relatively self-organising, this version does not require much supervision since the children create their own fun space.

To encourage a feeling and perception of connectedness, players then also colour in specially designed sheets containing twelve dots corresponding to the World System Model. This gets them into visually connecting different factors without having to give much explanation. The sheets encourage players to think about how many connections they could make between the dots in as many creative and colourful ways as possible. The aim of this step is to familiarise players with the idea of connectivity, the pattern of the World System Model and to have fun doing that. It proves to be a very popular activity with adults as well as children.

The stage of the game in which players gather around the circular layout is introduced as "we are the world". It begins with throwing and rolling balls (including an inflatable globe) and naming nodes in various combinations, moving as a group to the left or right a number of nodes, shouting the names as moves are made. This proves very engaging. Then simple connections are made between the nodes – the older children taking the lead, and using various physical means to demonstrate the link, from holding hands to hopping between nodes.

When the energy is high, participants are all asked to sit on their nodes for a story. This is ideally a story of the locality (in this case the history of the formation of the Calthorpe community) that the children and parents can identify with, woven between the nodes of the World System Model. This can be made visible and memorable by using string to connect the nodes together as the story unfolds (see Figure 3). The children enjoy guessing what the next node in the story is going to be by making their own connections. This is followed by standing again, holding the 'connections' and exploring various ways of moving over and under the strings. This links ideas of what matters in the connections with the physical pattern of the World Model.

Figure 3 *– Participants exploring the meaning of interconnections and the effects of changes in one node area on the others*

Feedback from the Calthorpe Project was very positive. Play workers who attended the Game were encouraging and had suggestions for other places where it would be a very welcome activity for children. One development from this kind of application could be the IFF World Game being permanently painted on the ground of children's play areas – 21st century hopscotch.

8: Strategy and Policy Development

There is rich potential for the World System Model and the associated IFF World Game to form the basis for a new strategic service: one that helps people to deal with levels of complexity and uncertainty that current strategy methods are too cumbersome and expensive to handle.

It is usually considered that strategy takes a long time to create and develop. In a fast-moving world, the strategic perspective tends to be sacrificed for operational survival. But this is simply a reflection of how our methods have not so far developed to deal with the new realities. We believe that the IFF World Game, augmented by some other strategic techniques, enables fast response to changing conditions without sacrificing strategic perspective and power. In other words, smart application of the World System Model and World Game will help create strategic resilience.

In this context, for example, we believe the IFF World Game is a technique more appropriate to 21st century conditions than scenario planning and conventional strategy analysis.

The structure and underlying research behind the World System Model provides the basis for short, sharp, strategic facilitation interventions that provoke a quantum leap in a client's strategic awareness and thinking. The potential for public sector organisations and commercial organisations is being explored, especially those with values of 'doing well by doing good'. The Scandinavian culture of *näringsliv*, for example, where business is treated as 'support for life', naturally demands a more holistic appreciation of the operating environment. There is also increasing evidence that city administrations the world over are becoming more committed to the idea of 'eco-cities'. In these and other settings, the IFF World Game offers a substantial tool for collective thinking and training for the world ahead.

An initial project to help frame a public health strategy was carried out with the UK National Health Service and showed that, used as a method to expand context awareness and strategic priorities, the approach works very well.

~Case Study 4~

Public Health Game: Tayside NHS - Reducing Health Inequalities

The IFF World Game was used as the central phase of a two-day strategy workshop aiming to generate a new approach to reducing health inequalities. The participants were the local team of public health consultants together with a range of practitioners and community representatives. After a briefing, the current situation was tested against the twelve nodes of the World System Model. From this work a set of four scenarios of possible futures was generated. The final Wisdom Council formed a set of declarations to serve as strategic guidelines. Further work was then done using a strategy mapping method to convert the declarations into an outline strategy over 10 to 15 years using the IFF 'Three Horizons' method.

Participant Feedback

"This not only generated a fresh strategic approach but the arguments were so convincing that we were able to persuade our colleagues who were not there."

"With relatively few amendments the strategy was approved by the Board. This we did not expect would happen so easily."

"The world model has helped us make the case to the Scottish public health community that broader and more comprehensive contextual thinking is essential to find ways to achieve our health and wellbeing goals."

~Case Study 5~

Island Regeneration: Clear Village Foundation - Integral Design

This game focused on a multi-dimensional approach to the regenerative and participatory design of a Mediterranean island (Pantelleria). Each of the twelve nodes was explored for its design relevance in relation to the present situation of the island, the aspirations of its mayor and community.

The outcome was a set of principles underpinning a comprehensive design brief that could guide the subsequent development of the project. These were derived from the final Wisdom Council declarations.

World Model Node	Declaration	Notes - It is essential to...
1: Wellbeing	Change through real sensing of the authenticity of actions – restoring meaning	Re-establish authenticity by considering the population's and visitors' ability to associate, recognise, understand and experience when faced with the measures/actions we plan. Authenticity restores meaning and creates a base for the fulfilment of human needs while moderating differences. Change has to be experienced by the senses – not merely rationally.
2: Food	Renaissance in local food growing that restores the soil	Cultivate a renaissance in the food growing culture after stimulating local conversations on what foods would be enjoyed and could be grown in a way that restores the soil and the natural beauty of the landscape in a changing climate.
3: Trade	Empower people (including youth) to become sustainable and entrepreneurial	Empower residents to become wise entrepreneurs focusing on sustainable and responsible businesses and including education opportunities for youth.

4: Energy	Ensure the renewable energy potential of the island is shared with the whole community	Develop a creative way to ensure that the benefits of Pantelleria's renewable energy potential are shared widely.
5: Climate	Develop an integrated adaptation plan which includes refugees	Develop and implement an integrated climate adaptation plan, move toward a non-carbon economy and prepare to plan to engage with refugees in order to adapt to the changing ecology, diversifying community and interdependent economy.
6: Biosphere	Broaden perspectives on participants and include all species and habitats	Broaden people's perspective on participants and invite the different species and natural habitats into the process.
7: Water	Develop multiple sources, health circles, effective regulation and application of alternative technologies	Follow a fourfold strategy of: 1. Develop multiple fresh water sources and protecting them 2. Initiate/extend health circles around significance of water 3. Awareness and distribution regulation 4. Research alternative technologies and embedded wisdom.

8: Habitat	Restore the destroyed environment that supports joyful living for all	Consider restoring the destroyed built environment so the island becomes again a place where people, of whatever colour and cultural background, enjoy living and working.
9: Wealth	Realise the unseen wealth that is present	Realise that there is wealth on the island, both seen and unseen.
10: Governance	Give voice to individual inhabitants by holding a large storytelling event	Invite all inhabitants to share their aspirations for the future of the island at a communal event of storytelling on the waterfront.
11: Community	Move from 'me' to 'we'; encourage sharing and multiplying	Go from 'me' to 'we': expand virtual limitations into infinite potential by sharing/multiplying.
12: Worldview	Seek unity in diversity - integrate European with African	Seek unity in diversity through programmes that embrace, celebrate and use the joint European and African heritage. This brings in the local/global. This unity can only be built upon social justice – so we must bring ethics back into decision-making.

~Case Study 6~

Local Authority Game: Cumbria County Council, UK -
Visioning the Future of Cumbria in a Changing World

Core challenge: Cumbria's thriving and resilient future – what direction, what shape and what needs to be done?

An IFF World Game played with a group of over 100 senior managers at Carlisle Racecourse. The World Game was designed to examine a particular set of local concerns – the flourishing and resilience of Cumbria – in the context of a rapidly changing world in which trends in many areas threaten to disrupt the future. The game was played as a drama in three acts:

Act 1 – The World of Concerns

In which we explore the twelve crucial areas for a viable planet, society, community, etc.

Act 2 – The Possible Futures

In which we anticipate interconnections between these trends, including synchronous failures.

Act 3 – The Wisdom Council Speaks

In which we tune into our collective intelligence and make declarations for far-sighted action.

In order to encourage an holistic and far-sighted conversation, participants were encouraged to think of themselves as members of a Special Commission appointed by the United Nations to consider the future sustainability and resilience of Cumbria as a model for other regions of the world. These are some of the recommendations that emerged:

Wellbeing: *Facilitate Community Self-Help.* Enable individuals, groups and communities to find their voice, communicate what their issues and priorities are, so that we can facilitate self-help.

Trade: *Local Solutions.* Recognise the diverse nature of Cumbria's people and communities and provide the infrastructure necessary to develop the respective strengths of those local communities.

Energy: *Cumbria the Renewable Capital of the UK.* Increase people's understanding of what they can do to use less energy and to become champions to make Cumbria the renewable capital of the UK using all of our natural resources – wood, wind, water and nuclear.

Climate: *Flexible Transport.* Managing expectations by working together with communities to reposition what is possible within our total set of local resources whilst maintaining communications infrastructure to support the economy, providing choice where possible, and utilising new and emerging technologies.

Biosphere: *Taking Care of Cumbria.* Channel the energy of every individual so they can play their part in taking care of Cumbria by reducing their impact on the environment.

Water: *Building Resilience, Meeting Needs.* Build resilience by helping communities and individuals help themselves. Pool resources and maximise delivery. Deliver progressively against need, targeting the most vulnerable first.

Habitat: *Housing Supporting Sustainable Communities.* Understand and plan for the types and volume of housing required by the communities of Cumbria; and ensure provision of healthy homes in recognition of housing's importance in an inclusive society.

Wealth: *Vibrant Cumbria.* Work with young people to find out what they want so they will stay or come, live and work and use their talents in Cumbria.

Governance: *Simplify Governance.* Simplified governance structure that provides clear leadership and empowers communities for the things that matter to them.

Community: *Empowering Communities to Make a Difference.* Develop communities that are flexible enough to meet demands and needs, recognise and take responsibility for their own potential growth, maximise the use of resources both local and national that are sustainable – this will create the reason for young people to stay and flourish in Cumbria. Additionally, in the context of community , a strong emphasis was given to:
Learning – a Bright Society. Change the future by diversifying provision, building on Cumbria's strengths, working together, improving social conditions to tackle inequality.

Worldview: *Economic Opportunity for the Young.* Reduce the current exodus of our young people by breaking down the barriers to partnership working in order to maximise economic stability and opportunity.

The total pattern of declarations gave the foundation for a shared vision of a thriving Cumbria that would build on its strengths and be realistic about the wider challenges that will inevitably arise in some form or another.

9: A Case Study - The Future of India

The World System Model can be a very useful tool for helping to think through an issue in the context of a changing world. This is also one of the main purposes of the World Game. Here, then, is a more detailed case study example (Case Study 7), showing how the Game can be played.

In February 2009, IFF facilitated a day-long World Game workshop with a leading economic research institute in India. The workshop involved the Institute's entire research staff, some 50 in all. It was held as part of the Institute's strategy development process and, therefore, focused on the Institute's central mission: **How to secure rapid, inclusive, sustainable growth in India over the next decade?**

As the group said: 'we have mastered the rapid part, but the inclusive and sustainable parts are proving problematic!'

In playing the Game, we used the same 3-act drama approach as we had in Cumbria (Case Study 6).

Act 1 – The World of Concerns

In which we explore the twelve crucial areas for a resilient society.

Act 2 – The Possible Futures

In which we anticipate challenges and opportunities

Act 3 – The Wisdom Council Speaks

In which we tune into our collective intelligence and make recommendations.

Getting to grips with the world

At the start of the day participants split into twelve small groups, one for each node of the World System Model. Each group was asked to study a written brief on global trends and discontinuities in that area (they were encouraged to draw on the IFF World System Model website and any other research material available to them). Each group identified the most troubling trend and the most troubling discontinuity in its node and assessed the potential impact of these on the core challenge of securing rapid, inclusive and sustainable growth for India. Out of that discussion they each identified a central concern for India.

At the close of this first research phase the facilitators called a meeting of the Indian cabinet. Role-playing within the World Game, one representative from each node delivered a short report to the Prime Minister as if attending a cabinet meeting to discuss the state of the world and its potential impact on India. Members of the group enjoyed getting into role – each trying to outbid the others with the depth of the challenge they could place on the Prime Minister's plate! The results of the exercise were remarkably candid and were captured in a vivid, visual display of hexagons showing the state of India in the world: a map of twelve interconnected trends, discontinuities and concerns.

Generating Scenarios – and far-sighted actions

Having explored the nodes of the World System Model and achieved a sense of the potential impact of changes in the global situation for India, the next stage of the World Game clustered the nodal groups together into four sets of three nodes. The purpose of this step was to start to take into account just some of the multiple connections between the nodes and to work deeper into the real complexity of the situation. (Any three will tend to spark interesting and illuminating conversations – drawing on the material already generated.)

The hexagon highlights from the first act now formed the substance for four clusters of issues, each based on three World Model nodes, as follows:

Worldview – Biosphere – Trade

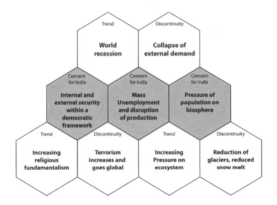

Wellbeing – Habitat – Energy

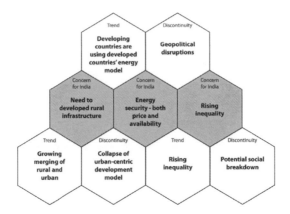

Governance – Food - Climate

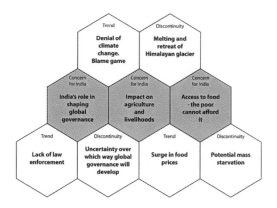

Wealth – Water – Community

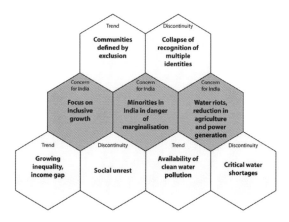

Figure 4 *– The three orange hexagons are concerns the group identified for the future of India. The yellow hexagons are the selected key trends and possible discontinuities or shocks to consider in their deliberations.*

Workshop participants formed a number of scenario groups based around these clusters of three issues. They were each asked to imagine a world of 'synchronous failure' – in which their set of three issues all impact at the same time or trigger each other in a cascade. This is rapid scenario generation. Any of the scenarios should be plausible, not fantastical, because ultimately the material links back to existing data and research.

In order to communicate a sense of these different futures to others, each group was invited to invent a number of headlines that might be anticipated in an Indian newspaper in that future; and also the titles of a number of academic articles they might imagine either reading or writing in that future.

Finally, having immersed themselves in their scenario in this way, the groups were invited to consider what 'far-sighted actions' might be adopted today in order either to ward off the threatened crisis or to enable swifter recovery in the event that it occurred (resilience). The four groups each enjoyed animated discussion and presented back some rich, varied and absorbing content. Some of the headlines offer a flavour:

- China diverts Brahmaputra River

- India pushes for food security in WTO

- Tourism revenues plummet

- Water riots throughout north India: tens of thousands killed

- The scholarly articles included:

- Fundamentalism and Economic/Industrial Performance: an Inter-state Comparison

- Growing affluence & conservatism: analysing the paradox

- Designing the visible hand for mitigating climate change for food security in India

There was also a rich agenda of potential 'far-sighted actions' – to be collated and considered later in light of the game as a whole. This second phase of the World Game was intended to have people enter more deeply into the complex global context so that they would get a sense of dealing with more of what is going on in the world than is normal. Thereafter, the intention was for participants to start turning the corner – from anticipating the worst to preparing for something better. That shift was captured in the final act of the game.

Wisdom Council

The final phase of the game was intended to draw on participants' capacity for taking an holistic perspective. We cannot analyse our way through the complexity of the World System Model, but we can game our way into it, experience it, and then draw on intuitive and collective intelligence to offer some deeply informed observations.

So, after lunch, twelve individuals were invited to form a Wisdom Council to sum up their learning from the game in the form of a set of declarations addressed personally to the Director of the Institute. Each of the twelve was invited to speak from a personal perspective, reflecting the insights of the group. They were to imagine that the Director was about to spend a short time with the Prime Minister: what should he stress as the most important areas that need attention for India now and over the next ten years?

The Wisdom Council first held a period of silence, to gather itself and to allow individuals to tune into the intelligence of the group. Then each of the twelve made a declaration. Other members of the group were invited to speak if there was anything of significance that had not been said. In conclusion, the Director offered his own reflections on what he had heard, and added his own dominant issues to the agenda.

This resulted in a list of 24 declarations – recorded below. Inevitably there are some overlaps.

Finally, since the day was also partly about aligning a group of individuals around an emerging strategy, everyone in the group was invited to consider the list of declarations and to decide in which areas the Institute could or should make a contribution. Everyone was given a single vote: and a condition of exercising it was that they should not only vote for an area of priority but also state the contribution they personally would be willing to make to the Institute's future work in that area.

The result of the voting is shown below:

No.	Summary of Declaration	Votes
1	Consider everything within its systemic context	-
2	Place our core focus internally	2
3	Complete Doha round and anti-protectionist declaration	1
4	Basic necessities available to all (e.g. health education, water)	-
5	Water and energy need more R&D and emphasis on how we make change	1
6	Access to credit for all, including the poor	2
7	Pay attention to equality and 'trickle down'	7
8	Tackle the social causes of fundamentalism	-
9	Progressive taxation for water	-
10	Tighter anti-corruption laws	3
11	Look for critical issues like labour law reform	2
12	Focus on governance linking local – national – global and build competence	8
13	Tackle shaming hunger and starvation in India, create universal access to food	-
14	Become more proactive in tackling climate change including using technology locally	-
15	Make long-term investment in social sectors (health, education, etc.) to reduce inequality, working with stakeholders	4
16	Address energy security by innovative diplomacy and providing energy for the poor	-
17	Invest in new renewable energy technologies, including through PPP	1
18	Develop strong institutional structures internally, including grassroots	1
19	Concentrate more on HOW to achieve objectives in a complex world	4

20	Reframe the concept of 'society' to include relationships with all other areas of the ecosystem	-
21	Explore practical alternatives to state redistribution of resources, e.g. income (how does 'trickle down' work in an Indian context?)	-
22	Pursue equity in all areas	-
23	Locate India in the world, e.g. global environment, global security	3
24	Align our agenda to personal purpose and engagement to make a real difference	2

By the end of an enjoyable, playful day, the staff of the Institute had engaged with a changing world in multiple dimensions and a very broad range of topics to inform research and had generated:

- a map of the landscape of concern for India over the next decade

- a rich menu of potential far-sighted policy actions in service of rapid, inclusive, sustainable growth

- a sense of priority focus areas for future strategy

- pages of detailed suggestions for how the Institute might address these, and offers of personal contribution and initiative to get things started.

Not a bad set of outcomes for something that started as 'only a game': thus illustrating the game as a supportive climate for creative thinking.

10: Creative Facilitation to Engage the World System

The World System Model occupies the interface between external systems and internal mental models. Experience and data from the external world is organised using the pattern of the Model. In turn, the Model, through gaming, reflection and application becomes internalised as part of people's mental furniture. This then helps people's 'carrying capacity' for complexity and interconnection.

Clearly the Model can be taken up as an aid to synthesis thinking and used in games, workshops and projects by groups interested in the concept and the process. However, in the matter of paradigm change, which by its nature is transformative, there is a whole range of psychological and group dynamic issues to be considered if its potential value is to be realised. It is useful to consider three levels of application task, level three being the most challenging. For each level there is a corresponding level of skill required of the facilitator.

Level of Application Task	Level of Facilitation
Level 1 – Operational	Applying the World System Model framework with current understanding and skills
Level 2 – Developmental	Having deeper training and skilling in the IFF-designed methods of use and gaming
Level 3 – Transformative	Having in-depth personal development and practice experience to take on intense transformational challenges

At level three, transformative change, the role of a suitable facilitator is crucial. The role at level three is not that of a trainer or a consultant, but someone who can help evoke the deep stories. The World Game provides an arena in which new stories of both the past and future can be crafted. Such new stories will be powerful if they take people beyond their familiar worldview and interpretations of the situation they are in. Playing such a facilitative role is not easy. Training or consulting are better known roles.

Will McWhinney characterised this third level as the 'Merlin' role. He describes this role not as the magician of the traditional stories but as "the sage that we encounter when we turn away from the everyday culture for guidance". Like Merlin, most such practitioners are by their role *liminal figures*, residing at the edge of organisations or society lest they be 'captured' as leaders, teachers or experts and reduced to levels two or one.

Depending at which level the World System Model is employed, there will be different patterns of usage and different effects.

In the Level 1 application, the form of the World System Model and the briefings associated with it (such as are provided on the IFF website) can be taken up and employed in a variety of ways. People can invent or apply their own methods for problem solving, running group sessions and developing a bigger-picture capability using these materials.

In Level 2 there needs to be an interest in, and an engagement with, alternative ways of viewing people and the world so that some of the deeper implications can be brought out. This depends on studying other IFF material and hopefully engaging in some events that are led by experienced people, at least to get a feel for those levels.

In Level 3, there is a need for an in-depth initiation into some of the foundational skills and insights generated by IFF that enable the more powerful and subtle aspects of the World System Model to be developed. At this level, the facilitator is really becoming part of the IFF community, contributing through practice and experience to the evolution of the methods and applications.

A skilled facilitator will have learned, through practice, how to work with groups in a multi-skilled way. The facilitator needs to understand the nature and complexity of the task that the user group is engaging in. This will enable the facilitator to guide the attention of the group to productive areas. The effectiveness of the World Game also depends on holding to the core designed processes. Any group will tend to deviate from these so the facilitator must bring them back to the main pathway. This guidance depends on the facilitator having mastered the Game's framework and its many variations – much easier if the principles of the World Game are well understood. Finally the facilitator needs to have experience and skill in dealing with some of the unconscious basic assumptions of any group that tend to frustrate achievement of the task, in other words successful completion of the Game. The more the group is challenged and stretched by the World Game, the more this last aspect is likely to be significant.

These factors are summarised in Figure 5.

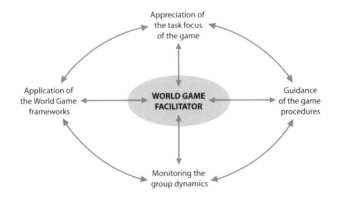

Figure 5 – *The basic skill structure for facilitating the World Game*

In IFF work we concentrate on a cooperative mode of facilitation. It is not hierarchical, in that the facilitator is not dominating the process, but more setting the scene and coaching people where necessary. In this case, the Model itself and the Game version do set a tight pattern that structures the processes for use or gaming. This is because, amongst other reasons, one object of the Model is to introduce ways of seeing connections that would not normally come out in a freewheeling session or application. So the cooperative mode is essentially between the IFF facilitator who holds the space and the culture of engagement, the group engaged in the process and their contributions, and the World System Model itself as an enabling framework.

In addition to the basic role of the facilitator there are supplementary techniques that are a helpful foundation for facilitating the IFF World Game.

Such tools alone will not in themselves bring about transformative change but can be useful in supporting a whole systems approach.

• *Holistic Mapping* – seeing the big picture

The natural environment consists of webs of relationships. Linkages connect the webs. Webs of relationships and linkages show up in our world as subtle and discernible patterns. It follows that thinking and planning should copy nature and emulate its natural coherence and strength. The ordinary spider's web serves as a useful example of unity and relationship in nature.

• *Generative Thinking* – going beyond a starting point

In generative thinking we seek to spark one idea off another and create something new. This is symbolised in the formula $1+1 = 3$. The creative result is more than the sum of its parts.

• *Systems Thinking* – recognising that effects can be causes

One of the severe limitations of current thinking about taking decisions is that of treating everything as if its behaviour were determined by linear causation. In both nature and human society many outcomes are determined by very complex interactions with feedback. Effects themselves become causes. This requires us to shift our worldview to include circles of causation that do not behave over time in the way we expect, extending or extrapolating from what we have seen so far.

• *Scenario Thinking* – anticipating multiple possibilities in the face of uncertainty

Complex situations have emergent properties that it is impossible to forecast or predict. The world situation is the most complete example of this complexity. Scenario thinking provides techniques for identifying critical variables and imagining different futures that might emerge, thus stimulating more options for resilience.

The World System Model can support many of these disciplines. In particular, given that we cannot successfully predict the emergent properties of complex systems, or their timing, we need to find ways to explore various hypotheses about what might happen. We will call this *anticipatory learning*. There are three basic forms this learning can take: action learning, learning games and pattern thinking.

Action learning[20] has several steps pursued in a recurring cycle. Each cycle adds to both experiential and theoretical learning. A typical cycle would be diagnosis of the situation, action planning, taking action, reviewing outcomes and re-appraising the situation. Where the action is aimed at improving, say, a design project or a policy development, the World System Model is partly a diagnostic tool and partly a basis for action planning.

The Model can also function as a basis for *collaborative learning games*. Collaborative learning games have several key design requirements:

1) To avoid a game degenerating to the point where one player makes the decisions of the team, there has to be a strong rationale for collaboration. The interactive complexity of the World System Model provides an arena where individually imposed solutions will not work.

2) To be engaging, the players need to care about the outcome and care that the outcome should be satisfying. Focusing the framework of the game on a challenge of locally owned concern is an important component of the game design.

3) To be sustainable and repeatable, the World Game needs to be different each time as the challenge evolves. The World Game is naturally focused on a changing world with new challenges emerging and these being seen and responded to differently as people gain new understandings.

Some of the characteristics of a learning game are that it challenges players to analyse situations, weigh evidence, set priorities and make choices. A learning game can also require the assimilation of new information and ideas as well as cooperation between fellow players. Of course, a game may also be competitive, but in the World Game the focus of competition is more on developing the capacity to cope with the complex and challenging world environment.

The World Game is a powerful way for people to develop and share *pattern thinking*. Most of our training in analysis and problem-solving focuses on the use of logic and the left brain. The World System Model, although based on cybernetic science, calls for right-brain pattern recognition and also imagination of futures which have not yet happened. Pattern thinking includes the ability to anticipate combinations of events, to connect symptoms to underlying causes, to recognise new options that emerge out of combinations and to devise strategies that take much more into account than can be achieved by analysis alone. Pattern thinking is also about the capacity to hold a more complex worldview in mind without strain.

11: A Platform for Planetary Learning

Civilisations have been at stake before, but there have always been other territories on the planet where alternative societies could flourish. This is no longer true. The only approaches worth considering are ones that encompass the whole planet.

The Stockholm Resilience Centre has researched and introduced the concept of planetary boundaries in different dimensions, e.g. carbon emissions, biodiversity and freshwater consumption. But environmental policy integration is in its infancy and there is no effective, planet-wide governance structure. It seems clear that more integrated modes of understanding and governance are urgently needed. These are difficult to achieve and will require much facilitation.

Given the previous millennium of predominantly analytical and increasingly reductionist worldviews – whether material, cultural or spiritual – it is no surprise that our attempts to deal with contemporary challenges are fragmented rather than integrated. We lack the skills and experience to apply holistic and interconnected methods suitable for a whole planet. However, such approaches are increasingly emerging and by much trial and error they may mature to a point of effectiveness. Many methods and experiments are needed. IFF is making its contribution to the emerging field under its guiding principle of *holism with focus.*

The World System Model can be used as a learning aid for interactive investigations of complex issues on any scale from family to whole planet. It does not provide answers (although it may do so in some respects as it is used and applied more widely) but challenges us to think differently. The model enables us to apply 'holism with focus' to a range of problematic areas, especially those that will not yield to conventional rational analysis.

So far we have barely begun to tap the potential of the Model, even as a simple scanning framework. Consider, for example, that a great deal of the information available on the state of the different nodes is very compartmentalised. So whilst, for example, we know plenty about the state of water in relation to both the biosphere and human needs, there is little clear discussion of the interconnectedness of these different factors.

The World System Model provides a framework to synthesise this information and map it into a form of patterned representation that offers an at-a-glance snapshot of the situation. An example is shown in Figure 6. Here the primary impact of interest is climate change. This is shown by the blue arrow. Each other node appears a different size according to the scale of the knock-on impact from climate change. In addition, the nodes that are affected are linked by red lines. Each red line raises a question as to what the mutual effect will be between this pair – a further level of analysis.

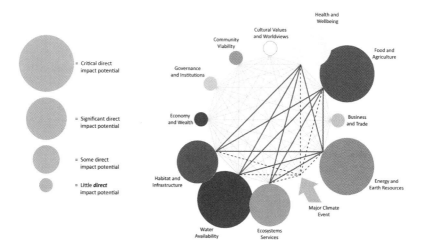

***Figure 6** – The World System Model showing degree of impact and possible knock-on effects*

In a rapidly changing world with high levels of uncertainty it is all too easy to stop considering long range futures because, if we cannot predict, anticipating the future is futile. Techniques of scenario planning have developed over the last three decades and have made their way closer to the mainstream of policy-making and strategic decision-making. However, the world as described in Chapter 1 is increasingly unsuited to scenario planning – which demands considerable resources and still often prioritises only two interacting discontinuities or synchronous failure potentials (the commonly used 2 x 2 scenario grid).

Experiments have been made using the World System Model as a substitute for scenario planning as a much quicker way to 'wind tunnel' policies and strategies in a variety of possible future conditions. 'Wind tunnelling' here refers to the technique of projecting an intention, policy or strategy into several distinct views of the future and asking a variety of 'what if?' questions. The exercise is a kind of imaginative simulation of what might be and what effect it might have on the success or failure of the intention, policy or strategy.

Case Study 7, in Chapter 9, illustrated one application of this approach, using the World Game, in India. Case Study 8 shows how the World System Model can be used to review large amounts of data on global climate change and provide a tool for rapid comparison and assessment in policy discussions.

~Case Study 8~

Impact of Climate Change: Second Order Climate Change Impact

The World System Model has been used to help organise an overview of the global impact of climate change as part of an investigation of the vulnerability of the UK to global climate change. This required:

- First, devising a way to summarise the potential impact of climate change in most land areas of the Earth.

- Secondly, estimating the vulnerability of those areas. This meant finding proxies to estimate the adaptive capacity of the societies in those areas.

- Finally, investigating the interdependencies of the UK with those areas, in order to help identify where the exposure to secondary impacts might be.

Using the World System Model approach made it easier to examine the data for second order impacts of climate change – i.e. where the impact of climate change has further repercussions for other forms of interdependency, such as health, trade or food supply.

This review developed a set of systems maps using the World System Model on the lines of Figure 6 that summarise important linkages and consequences that flow from potential climate impacts in the world[21].

Overall, synthesis literature covering eighteen regions and countries of the world was reviewed for the current best estimates of potential climate impact over the next half century. Profiles were created of each of these regions so that the strength of any given impact and its connection with other impacts (for example the links between impact of climate change on water, food and wellbeing) could be easily seen.

A deeper study searched for evidence of how these interconnections have been noticed by researchers and thus compiled a unique database of extracts from the literature that highlights the considerable interconnectedness of the different aspects of the World System Model.

Some conclusions from this study are incorporated into the UK Foresight report: *The International Dimensions of Climate Change.*[22]

The approach promises to be useful for horizon-scanning, analysis, review and policy prioritisation.[23]

The study of, and research into, interconnections is the next big challenge for both scientists and policy-makers. In Chapter 2 the nature of synchronous failure was explained. The question here is how to monitor trends and events in a combinatorial way that may alert us more rapidly to emerging synchronous events, or 'perfect storms'. Equally, in our search for solutions that increase our resilience we need also to look at situations in different nodes *in combination*. IFF is currently working on a project to create a tool kit and a process for carrying out both these tasks with greater effectiveness. This project is called a 'Platform for Planetary Learning'. The word 'learning' is important in this context because it emphasises that we have never been here before and our best chance is to increase the depth and speed of our learning.

Overall, the World System Model offers a framework to organise scanning, make judgements about what is significant and place any item in a larger context. As it is used in this way, the material that is accumulated through the scanning function becomes a resource for continuous updating of the World System Model node briefings, and therefore for the IFF World Game.

The first generation of the World System Model (the one described in this book) concentrates on the range of trends and discontinuities that threaten global or local sustainability and require the development of resilience or adaptive capacity. The next generation, which is currently under development (and which is illustrated in the climate impact work in

Case Study 8 above), extends the framework to include an emphasis on visioning possible futures for humanity in the context of one-planet living. This includes ways of gaining an integrated picture of the various transition initiatives that are taking us in that direction.

Here we are using the three horizons framework[24] shown in Figure 7. With the three horizons as a backcloth, the model can act as a way of orchestrating and interpreting diverse data about current and future trends.

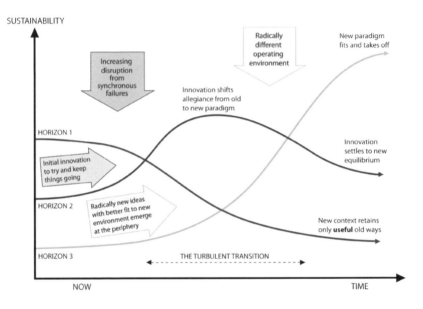

Figure 7 – *The three horizons of world transformation*

In this framework, Horizon 1 is continuing as we are: business as usual. If left alone, conditions will inevitably decline, leading to disruption and, *in extremis*, extinction. The vision is referred to as Horizon 3. It has the potential to displace Horizon 1. However, the future cannot be well known; it is emergent. So Horizon 3 must remain a shaping vision rather than a predictive one. The tough challenge is the transition that we call Horizon 2, in which we experiment, invent and pioneer alternatives. Some will succeed, some will fail, some will be hijacked to prop up the declining system and some will be effective beyond expectation.

Once the non-viability of the Horizon 1 system (the *status quo*) is seen more clearly without avoiding or denying the issues, the question naturally arises: "is there a viable alternative?" Thus we seek a vision of a better state of affairs, (Horizon 3), in which the dislocations and disruptions are replaced by viable alternatives. However, these alternatives, in the context of an holistic view, cannot achieve success in isolation and disregarding the overall complex of interactions. The vision as well as the diagnosis must be holistic. Supposing a vision that is viable in all dimensions is possible, then we face the challenge of transition and transformation: Horizon 2.

The World System Model can take a different form for each horizon: the present diagnosis (Horizon 1), the vision of viability and sustainability (Horizon 3) and innovative and turbulent transition, namely Horizon 2. These are symbolised in Figure 8.

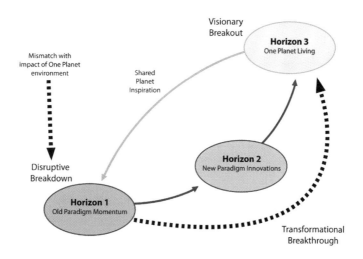

Figure 8 *– The impact of visioning in the transition to one-planet living*

In its Horizon 1 form, the World System Model assembles most of the main reasons – global trends and discontinuities – why 'business as usual' is not going to work in a rapidly changing world that exceeds the planetary carrying capacity.

The Horizon 2 version assembles and integrates an overview of the positive innovations and changes that can help in transition. It especially addresses the idea of synchronous solutions which, in the spirit of Buckminster Fuller's anticipatory design science, aim to achieve more and more with less and less.

The Horizon 3 version is a vision of the parameters of the good life that can be sustainable and resilient and offer a viable form of one-planet living. As such, it will offer a critique of any living arrangement in whatever value system, culture or geographical location in terms of both local sustainability and the sustainability of the planet as a whole.

The World System Model, fully developed, thereby becomes a platform for planetary learning. Its value lies in providing a common orientation and understanding of the planetary context shared by leaders and communities in any society, in any nation and in any culture. Since there is only one sustainable option for us all – namely one-planet living – this will become a far better basis for living than the doctrine of quasi infinite economic growth or that of domination by one fundamentalist belief system.

The experiments conducted so far show that the framework, suitably adapted, can be effective with children, with communities, with professional organisations, with city and even national administrations as well as taking a total planet view on issues treated at any level. It is, effectively, a foundation for active, engaged, global citizenship.

It counteracts the centuries of conditioning of analytical thought which reduces and fragments the whole into disconnected parts. As the children's nursery rhyme points out, "all the king's horses and all the king's men couldn't put Humpty together again." The World System Model works by appealing to the pattern thinking inherent in the brain, evoking confidence in our capacity for holistic understanding and thereby rapidly developing the capacity to see vital interconnections.

There is also a psychological factor at work: our capacity to hold items in short-term memory is reckoned to be 7 plus or minus 2. However, the power of a visual mental image is that it can compensate to some extent for this limitation. In this model we are assisted to hold in mind twelve interconnected factors and review up to sixty-six of those connections. It also acts as a spur to apply the creative thinking principle 'consider all factors'.

The Model acts as a framework for searching out and positioning relevant knowledge. It is a kind of safety net for significant factors that can so easily 'fall through the cracks' between the main bodies of information about each node. Many examples of this emerge in the course of playing the World Game, where the dialogues that are stimulated on connections between the nodes throw up new questions and insights.

The interactions between people stimulated by the World Game or by the use of the World System Model as a technique for strategic thinking also cultivate the art of judgement, especially about the significance of information. In a world of information explosion and communication overload this aspect is very important. Understanding does not arise from simply being informed but requires mental digestion and the positioning of information in a larger pattern. In using the system model in groups, people learn to find common ground for judgement. This is especially important for one-planet solutions, which by their very nature must be interdisciplinary.

Once people have internalised the World System Model, either through working with it or playing with it, it begins to function cognitively as a way of rapidly assimilating and positioning information. For example, there are innumerable web sites which scan and compile information on what is happening, latest developments and recent scientific findings and interpretations. For someone interested in grasping the whole picture, this plethora of detail can be experienced as information overload.

But using the World System Model as a combination of web portal and framework for systemic understanding, the task of maintaining holism with focus becomes much easier. When supported by suitably configured software, the Model becomes a framework for managing information around the twelve nodes and their interconnections; and around the three horizons of diagnosis, vision and promising transition pathways. This data-rich environment is then no longer an overwhelming mass of information: it becomes a platform for planetary learning. Importantly, the inclusion of worldview as one of the nodes of the model invites a balanced perspective (protagonists of a single worldview tend to dominate decisions about what information is important and what it means). To be effective, the creation of this platform for planetary learning should become an open source project for all global citizens. This could then further support the themes of this book: visioning for one-planet living, building transformative resilience and getting 'ready for anything'.

12: Ready for Anything: Transformative Resilience

This book is about realising the goal of all resilience planning: to be ready for anything without planning for everything. I have shown in previous chapters how the World System Model and the IFF World Game can be used in a variety of settings to advance that aim. Finally, I would like to offer some thoughts on how to frame the goal itself: transformative resilience.

We might start with a standard definition of a resilient community:

> *A resilient community is one that takes intentional action to enhance personal and collective capacity to sustain the good life in the context of turbulence and disruption to its optimum living arrangements.*

This is fine so far as it goes. But our analysis of potential conditions such as synchronous failure shows that 'life-as-usual' no longer has the degree of resilience required – even if we could restore it after a serious shock. We have to question whether the capacity simply to 'bounce back' is enough.

We must, therefore, define two levels of resilience. The first level is *Status Quo Resilience* which is the capacity to recover from disruption back to the 'life-as-usual' level. The second level is *Transformative Resilience* which is the capacity to shift to a new system capable of absorbing and bouncing back from more persistent disruption.

This is a new level of adaptive capacity, 'bounce beyond', which becomes possible when human communities restructure their specific localities with a new sensitivity to the unique ecological conditions (opportunities and limits) of place and in full awareness of their regional and global context. This is what the World System Model is designed to help bring about. Transformative resilience is about intelligent, humble, and scale-sensitive co-creation between human communities and the wider ecological communities they inhabit.

As noted in Chapter 3, the point of inserting the term 'good life' in the above definition of resilience is that our views and experiences of the good life become completely and subconsciously enmeshed in our daily lives so that we are unaware of our assumptions. This means that, when confronted by the need to change these assumptions, people feel aggrieved that they are being required to give up the 'good life'.

This is where the idea of the third horizon (see Chapter 11) comes into play. To achieve 'bounce beyond' we need a vision of what that 'beyond' might be like. This is why the term *visioning* has been introduced as a strong, affirmative way of orientating towards the future. *What is actually needed is to reframe the essence of the good life in a new system of living.* Evidence is accumulating that changes towards greater resilience, rather than diminishing, actually increase the capacity for a new type of good life. We will call this capacity transformative resilience.

Transformative Resilience

In order to understand transformative resilience we need to build it up through different levels of resilient structure. There are basically four levels.

The first is the kind of resilience that engineers design in mechanistic systems. The system is designed so that when it is disrupted from a steady state it will return to that state as quickly as possible. In this way the efficiency of the system is maintained in changing circumstances. This kind of resilience places limitations on the degree of disruption it can stand. For example a building designed to withstand earthquakes will have some degree of flexibility built in to absorb the shock. It will not be built in a brittle way. However, there could be an earthquake of a magnitude that exceeds those limits and the building does not recover or even collapses.

The second kind of resilience is usually seen in basic ecological systems, which are more complex and interactive than mechanistic systems. They have an inherent capacity to restore themselves after shocks. For example a biome might be temporarily flooded in extreme weather but rapidly recover its equilibrium when the flood subsides. Ecological systems also have the capacity to evolve towards higher levels of complexity and resilience. Human attempts in desert restoration can accelerate and aid the natural process of succession by introducing systems-enhancing species that in turn attract flora and fauna that were not previously present in that environment.

The third kind of resilience shows itself in ecological systems over longer cycles of change and enables the system to renew itself constantly.

A system with this kind of resilience is not only able to absorb disturbances but also goes through a recurring renewal cycle, which has four main stages. As the diverse species in the ecosystem adapt to the opportunities presented by different ecological niches in their environment, their individual populations grow (*growth phase*). After a time they reach certain limits, for example in terms of space and nutrients, and enter a *conservation phase* when very few resources are freely available. This phase eventually collapses and releases the concentrated materials in the system and breaks much of the coupling (e.g. complexity of the food-web) in the *release phase*. Following on from this stage a *reconfiguration phase* is possible; this more or less re-establishes the original vitality.

The fourth kind of resilience, transformative resilience, is found in a very specific kind of socio-ecological system: a human-ecological system that has transformative capacity. This system not only absorbs and adapts to disturbance but can *anticipate and heed* future impending disturbances and reconfigure itself to increase its capacity to bounce back after shock.

This transformation also follows the fourfold cycle of growth, conservation, release and reconfiguration. The difference is that, in the reconfiguration stage, innovations have been prepared and are introduced that change the nature of the system. This means that the next growth and expansion stage is taking place on different foundations. This is the meaning of Graham Leicester's words in the Preface: 'planning for anything without planning for everything'. Transformative resilience, then, requires some capacity to anticipate future events and the capacity to see the implication for the future of unexpected disruption. It does not fall into the pattern of 'when things return to normal' but, instead, creates a new normal.

Transformative resilience therefore enables a number of characteristics:

- Adaptation to irreversible changes
- Core restructuring processes at different levels
- Gaining needed resources from multiple sources
- Increase of variety and diversity in the system
- Generation of a wide range of options
- Having a sustained memory of the past and a consciously created 'memory of the future'

- Scale-sensitive linkage of its own subsystems and wider linkages with larger systems in its environment that contain it

- Accumulating the surplus energy to make a leap to a different level of 'normal'

In the circumstances of the contemporary world, we believe we must aim always for transformative resilience – bounce back will not be enough, we must 'bounce beyond'.

We hope that the ideas in this book and particularly the framework of the World System Model and the processes developed around the World Game will make a significant contribution to this goal.

Summary

To sum up the practical implications of this book:

First, I have shown how the World System Model provides a framework for developing a new capacity to be aware of our world in an interconnected way, counteracting decades of trying to manage complexity by splitting everything up into supposedly 'manageable' component parts.

Second, I have shown how the IFF World Game provides a rapid and economical way for groups, whether they be communities, experts, researchers or policy-makers, to understand and address the complex challenges arising from the interaction of global and local situations.

Third, I have suggested that the World System Model helps orchestrate horizon-scanning to develop foresight based on the integration of current best science and values-driven visioning of desirable futures that can sustain one-planet living.

Fourth, I have suggested that coupling this approach with the methods of the wisdom council provides a way to co-create the capacity to be 'ready for anything', to develop transformative resilience.

All this is possible. But it cannot happen if we stay in denial or persist in complacency, or imagine that our current assumptions are smart enough to deal with all the contingencies we face.

Aesop has a cautionary tale to remind us of the shortcomings of our current assumptions:

The One-Eyed Doe

> *A doe blind in one eye was accustomed to graze as near*
> *to the edge of the cliff as she possibly could, in the hope*
> *of securing her greater safety. She turned her sound eye*
> *towards the land that she might get the earliest tidings of the*
> *approach of hunter or hound, and her injured eye towards*
> *the sea, whence she entertained no anticipation of danger.*
> *Some boatmen sailing by saw her, and taking a successful*
> *aim, mortally wounded her. Yielding up her last breath, she*
> *gasped forth this lament: "O wretched creature that I am!*
> *To take such precaution against the land, and after all to*
> *find this seashore, to which I had come for safety, so much*
> *more perilous. You cannot escape your fate!"*

It may be that we cannot escape our fate either. But we are certainly not going to improve our chances by turning a blind eye to the complex challenges facing us in the years ahead.

I hope the World System Model, the IFF World Game and its associated platform for planetary learning will make some small contribution to giving us the foresight and the vision to meet them with confidence: to be ready for anything.

Acknowledgements

The development of a complex concept and practical technique around the World System Model idea would be impossible without collaboration. The range of influences on my development of this approach is many and diverse.

I would like to single out Graham Leicester, Director of International Futures Forum for unflagging support and patience; Andrew Lyon for his courageous pioneering of applications; Daniel Wahl for his meticulous and knowledgeable critique; Rebecca Hodgson for her supportive research on the vast complexities of world trends and helping to distil them down; Alexandra Hodgson for help with the graphics as well as important application concepts; my wife, Liz, for her encouraging suggestions; Bill Sharpe and Ian Page who have shared many sessions with me wrestling the meaning out of complexity; Maureen O'Hara for her deep insight into psychological responses to high anxiety situations; Napier Collyns of GBN and IFF for his constant encouragement to communicate this work; Frances Tait and Ragne Griffin for demanding clarity from my sketchy drafts; and all those who have participated in IFF World Games and thereby helped evolve the Game's applicability.

Without the vision and encouragement of Gary Chicoine I would not have had the background and the mental stamina to take this work on. My special thanks to Matthew Fairtlough of Triarchy Press who has made publication possible. Much gratitude also to Andew Carey for his supportive editing of my efforts to express clearly this complex field.

Anthony Hodgson
Pitlochry, 2011

Bibliography

Beddington, John, *Food, Energy, Water and the Climate: A Perfect Storm of Global Events?*, London: Government Office for Science, 2009

Beer, Stafford, *Platform for Change*, Chichester: John Wiley, 1994

Blackmore, Christine, *Learning to Appreciate Learning Systems for Environmental Decision Making: A 'Work-in-Progress' Perspective*, Systems Research and Behavioural Science 22, 329-341, 2005

Brown, V.A, Harris, J.A. and Russell, J.Y., *Tackling Wicked Problems Through the Transdisciplinary Imagination*, London: Earthscan, 2010

Curry, Andrew and Hodgson, Anthony, 'Seeing in Multiple Horizons: Connecting Futures to Strategy', *Journal of Futures Studies*, Volume 13, Number 1, 2008

Heinberg, Richard, *The End of Growth*, Gabriola Island: New Society Publishers, 2011

Homer-Dixon, Thomas, *The Upside of Down – Catastrophe, Creativity and the Renewal of Civilisation*, London: Souvenir Press, 2006

King, Alexander and Schneider, Bertrand, *The First Global Revolution*, New York: Simon and Schuster, 1991

McWhinney, Will, *Paths of Change – Strategic Choices for Organizations and Society*, London: Sage, 1992

Meadows, Donella, Randers, Jorgen and Meadows, Dennis, *Limits to Growth – The 30-Year Update*, White River Junction, VT: Chelsea Green, 2004

Michael, Donald, *In Search of the Missing Elephant*, Axminster: Triarchy Press, 2010

Pontin, John and Roderick, Ian, *Converging World*, Totnes: Green Books, 2007

Revans, Reg, *ABC of Action Learning*, Aldershot: Gower, 2011

Rockström, J., *et al.*, *Planetary Boundaries: A Safe Operating Space for Humanity*, Stockholm: Stockholm Resilience Centre, 2009

Sachs, Jeffrey, 'The Deepening Crisis: When Will We Face the Planet's Environmental Problems?', *Scientific American*, September 1, 2010

Seiden, Lloyd Steven, *Buckminster Fuller's Universe*, Cambridge: Perseus Publishing, 1989

Sharpe, Bill and van der Heijden, Kees (Eds), *Scenarios for Success*, Chichester: John Wiley, 2007

The Author

Anthony Hodgson is the founder of Decision Integrity Limited, a company pioneering ways to facilitate better decisions through the application of holistic thinking, systems mapping, integrative group processes and sustainable values.

His career-long consulting experience spans public, private and voluntary sectors in the UK and farther afield, from Hewlett Packard and Statoil to the UK National Health Service.

A graduate of the Royal College of Science, Imperial College, London, Tony has taught on the Executive MBA at The London Business School on Visual Thinking and Team Learning and on an elective programme, 'The Art and Science of the Long View'. He helped facilitate the foundation of SOL International (the Society for Organisational Learning). He is a founder member of the International Futures Forum (where he is World Modelling Research Coordinator). He is also researching new ways of thinking about the future and acting in the present at the Centre for Systems Studies in the University of Hull, UK.

Tony has published papers on various aspects of educational technology, systems thinking and facilitation, co-authored two books on Scenario Thinking and has contributed to a book on Cybernetics and Management. International Futures Forum

International Futures Forum

International Futures Forum (IFF) is a non-profit organisation established to support a transformative response to complex and confounding challenges and to restore the capacity for effective action in today's powerful times.

At the heart of IFF is a deeply informed inter-disciplinary and international network of individuals from a range of backgrounds covering a wide range of diverse perspectives, countries and disciplines. The group meets as a learning community as often as possible, including in plenary session. And it seeks to apply its learning in practice.

IFF takes on complex, messy, seemingly intractable issues – notably in the arenas of health, learning, governance and enterprise – where paradox, ambiguity and complexity characterise the landscape, where rapid change means yesterday's solution no longer works, where long-term needs require a long-term logic and where only genuine innovation has any chance of success.

The Publishers

Triarchy Press publishes good books in the field of organisational and social praxis. Praxis is the cyclical process by which we apply theories and skills in practice, reflect on our experience, refine those theories and skills, and then apply them again in practice.

We look for the best new thinking on the organisations and social structures we work and live in. And we explore the most promising new practices in these areas. We look, in particular, for writers who can provide a bridge between academic research/theory and practical experience. Our books cover innovative approaches to designing and steering organisations, the public sector, teams, society... and the creative life of individuals.

Our partnership with IFF gives us the privilege of working with some of the most inspiring writers, thinkers and practitioners in the field. They challenge us to embrace the potential of change rather than retreat into the familiar, opening the door to wiser preparation for an uncertain future.

Other books published by Triarchy in partnership with IFF include:

Ten Things to Do in a Conceptual Emergency
Fresh and insightful thinking to help us take more effective and responsible action in a world we do not understand and cannot control.

Transformative Innovation in Education
Based on IFF's work in Scotland to turn the Curriculum for Excellence into a practical instrument for educational transformation.

Economies of Life
There are many economies. Only one is based on money but all bring richness to our lives. This book uses ecological thinking to re-examine the terms 'economy' and 'value', to consider what keeps each economy healthy and to see how they can support innovation and sustainability.

In Search of the Missing Elephant
Five extraordinary and challenging essays by Don Michael, whose wisdom, humanity, integrity, and commitment to confronting the most vexing and complex problems continue to inspire everyone who encounters his work.

To find out more, buy a book, write for us or contact us, please visit:

www.triarchypress.com

Triarchy Press

Notes

1   IFF is the International Futures Forum. For more information, see the endpages and the IFF website at: http://bit.ly/tp_IFF

    For the World System Model, see: http://bit.ly/tpWORLDMOD

2   *Living Planet Report 2010*, Biodiversity, biocapacity and development, WWF International: http://bit.ly/tp2010LPR

3   Rockström *et al.*, 2009

4   For the IFF World Game, see: http://bit.ly/tpWORLDGAME

5   See Note 2

6   *Millennium Ecosystem Assessment, Living Beyond Our Means - Natural Assets and Human Wellbeing*: http://bit.ly/tpMEA

7   Homer-Dixon, 2006

8   Beddington, 2009: http://bit.ly/tpSTORM

    "There is an intrinsic link between the challenge we face to ensure food security through the 21st century and other global issues, most notably climate change, population growth and the need to sustainably manage the world's rapidly growing demand for energy and water. It is predicted that by 2030 the world will need to produce 50 per cent more food and energy, together with 30 per cent more available fresh water, whilst mitigating and adapting to climate change. This threatens to create a 'perfect storm' of global events."

9   O'Hara, Maureen, 'Crisis and Opportunity' (slide) in *The Academy in Powerful Times*: http://bit.ly/tpMOHA

10 Geoffrey Vickers quoted in Blackmore, 2005

    "My second and allied anxiety is that the new conceptual revolution, by multiplying our power to make models and our habit of using them, may also magnify our confidence in the models we make and may equally reduce our confidence in our power to know any reality we cannot explicitly model. The clear message of systems thinking is that human scope is limited and that we cannot use even what scope we have except in a situation in which we are sensitively and intimately

engaged. We have been offered this insight and the temptation to
ignore it and vested interests powerfully favour the second. This we
should avoid both as a duty and as a vital interest of our society. For if
I am right, we can know more, as well as less than we can model and
we shall be doubly hampered, even by comparison with our present
plight, if we overrate our models and underrate ourselves."

11   Michael, 2010

12   For more on The Resilience Alliance, see: http://bit.ly/tpRESIL

13   Heinberg, 2011

14   Meadows *et al.*, 2004

15   Jeffrey Sachs (2010) talks about this in detail:

"We are losing not just time but the margin of planetary safety,
as the world approaches or trespasses on various thresholds of
environmental risk. With the human population continuing to rise
by 75 million or more per year and with torrid economic growth in
much of the developing world, the burdens of deforestation, pollution,
greenhouse gas emissions, species extinction, ocean acidification and
other massive threats intensify…

What deep features of our national and global socioeconomic
processes cause these repeated failures? First, the risks to
sustainability are truly unprecedented in their global scale and have
come upon society rather suddenly in the past two generations.
Second, the problems are scientifically complex and involve enormous
uncertainties. Not only must public opinion catch up with reality, but
key sciences must also scramble to measure, assess and address the
new challenges."

16   http://bit.ly/tpWORLDMOD

17   See Note 6

18   Available from 2012

19   Brown *et al.*, 2010

20   The basis of action learning, summarised by its originator Reg Revans, is: *"Learning involves doing... Since action learning suggests that we may best master whatever unknown challenge appears by working with others who seek to triumph in the same way, its programmes should be collectively designed and launched by those who hope to profit from them."* For a full explanation of action learning see Revans, 2011.

21   The reports are available for download at: http://bit.ly/tpCLIMATE

22   *The International Dimensions of Climate Change*: http://bit.ly/tpINTDIM

23   See the study: *The Impact of Climate Impact, Books 1 and 2* at the IFF website.

24   Curry & Hodgson, 2008